THE CORPSES OF THE FUTURE

A little after, the stream that I was following fell into
the Tarn at Pont de Montvert of bloody memory.
— Robert Louis Stevenson

THE CORPSES OF THE FUTURE

LYNN CROSBIE

ANANSI

Published in Canada in 2017 and the USA in 2017 by House of Anansi Press Inc.
www.houseofanansi.com

House of Anansi Press is committed to protecting our natural environment. As part of our efforts, the interior of this book is printed on paper made from second-growth forests and is acid-free.

21 20 19 18 17   1 2 3 4 5

Library and Archives Canada Cataloguing in Publication

Crosbie, Lynn, 1963-, author
The corpses of the future / Lynn Crosbie.

Poems.
Issued in print and electronic formats.
ISBN 978-1-4870-0091-2 (hardback).—ISBN 978-1-4870-0090-5 (paperback).—
ISBN 978-1-4870-00929 (html)

I. Title.

PS8555.R61166C67 2017   C811'.54   C2016-901603-X
                               C2016-901604-8

Library of Congress Control Number: 2016958369

Cover design: Alysia Shewchuk
Cover photograph: Lynn Crosbie

We acknowledge for their financial support of our publishing program the Canada Council for the Arts, the Ontario Arts Council, and the Government of Canada through the Canada Book Fund.

Printed and bound in Canada

This book is dedicated to my father, Douglas James Crosbie.

To my mother, Heather; my brother James and my sister Mary.

a dolore teneantur

CONTENTS

傷
感

SEPTEMBER 11, 2016. I starting writing this book a year after my father lost his vision and was diagnosed with frontotemporal dementia. He had fallen down the basement stairs on November 17, 2013, in the Pointe-Claire house he lived in with my mother for thirteen years, and was taken to the Jewish General. He had incurred a bad concussion; after examining the X-rays, the doctors at the General said he could go home. My father protested, saying he felt too ill. He was then transferred to a rehab (an *hébergement*) called the Solomon House, in Snowdon. There, my parents were informed he would have to wait until April (five months) for an MRI, and they, uneasily, elected to leave. They returned home, although his pain was terrible. He phoned me, anxiously, several times a day, drove to various doctors who would not see or treat him, until he was so sick he could not get out of bed. My mother soon called another ambulance, which brought him back to the General. He was operated on immediately, as his brain was bleeding and had been for some time. During the operation, he suffered two small strokes in the periorbital region of his brain. He awoke terrified and blind, but lucid. The surgeon who operated tersely told me it was not his fault and, within a couple of weeks, bluntly refused to speak to me at all. Quickly after the operation, dementia latched on, and my father was bounced from one chintzy CHSLD Vigi[1] to another. He became increasingly violent. The various staffs matched his violence with medieval restraints, and overmedication. He was brought to the Douglas from the Lachine *hébergement* (where he resides still) for

---

1   *Vigi Santé est une entreprise familiale qui, depuis plus de 35 ans, a à cœur le bien-être des personnes hébergées. Grâce à ses efforts continus pour assurer la prestation de soins et de services de qualité, l'organisation se situe aujourd'hui parmi les chefs de file dans le domaine de la gériatrie au Québec.*

evaluation. There, after a terrible wait and no assistance — the CNIB have done next to nothing, to date — an ethical doctor agreed to view his problems in an informed way. After Dad returned to Lachine, the restraints were banned and his medications were lowered, significantly. The staff here is good, some are very kind. But it is still a violent ward, filled with screaming and moaning — often by the locked, heavy door that leads outside. My father cannot have a telephone; my mother brings her cell-phone on her twice-daily visits, and my siblings and I speak to him then. Some days he can see distant objects: his vision is largely gone.

These poems acted, for over two years, as a way of processing what I came to think of as the symbolic language of dementia, and of course as a way of remembering *for* my father. The dates are not always correct, and there is a bit of time/space confusion; the narrative is best understood as an account of my visits and talks with my dad, and as a corollary to his profound illness.

The trauma resulting from this disease, and from his loss of vision, for my father, and for us, his family, is enormous.

"The corpses of the future" is one of my father's remarks, as is "stinky little blankets" and more. I indicate in the book that I took notes, and there are very many. I hope that I have made it clear when he is speaking, in a book that amounts to a collaboration between us.

I stopped writing the poems in the beginning of 2016. But I still reach for my notes when he talks about his new horses, Wind and Thunder, black and brown stallions; about his recording contract; of missing things (his cats, wallet, old friends); and when he makes excellent observations, such as, "Show me one dead person who's still alive."

I wrote this book to feel closer to my father, to better understand him as well as the illness that often keeps him away from us in a region I can access only through the parole of dreams and poetry and lies.

— Lynn Crosbie

PEEWEE

It is August: my father is alive and poised to leave the third centre he has been placed in, between hospital stays, since the beginning of this year.

His doctor tells me that his diagnosis has changed again, from vascular to frontotemporal dementia, both of which are fatal.

He is headed for the Douglas, a mental institution I grew up fearing and the subject of countless casual assessments among friends, as in

She belongs in the Douglas — the lady with the slate-grey beehive wearing a shower curtain in the Roman fashion, and checkerboard Vans.

She was the mother of my childhood friend. My mother and I watched the police muscle her into a paddy wagon, as she struggled and smoked

And said, of all of us, *Regardez mes voisins, voyez comme ils rient!*
while my mother's beautiful face bathed in tears.

It has been long enough that my sister, brother or I slip up and say Mom's house, or Mom's money — left with nothing, she sleeps fitfully, gets up,

Having packed a bag with wax-paper-wrapped peanut butter sandwiches, magazines, change for the Tuck Shop, a ruby-red apple,

She gets into her old car and drives, back and forth all day, which makes my father alternately irritated and infatuated.

The days, each of our days, are rated according to his mood:
a good day means that he ate well, and talked companionably before falling asleep.

On bad days, he is sedated.

Doped up and beyond wanting, he sees desire for what it is, the dead body of a whore *(qui) moisit parmi les ossements,*

His vanishing diamondbird.

When we spoke yesterday, he cried because I am his child, and he misses me.
Today he told me to buzz off and flicked the phone at my mother

Because I didn't understand the sequence of numbers he recited,
192 – 24–22,

And would not find his childhood peewee team and kill them.
Please, would you listen to me? They have to die.

I do not know, and likely never will, what these kids did to my
strong, shy father.

But for one lurching moment, I see myself reaching backwards and
lining them up; using handkerchiefs as blindfolds and bindings,

And executing them in a panoramic sweep or, at least,
shooting their hands and knees, I would tell them,

This is your fault, you heartless monsters!
as the blood retched into puddles.

I would splash through them, towards my speechless father, calling,
Eleven down.

BLOOD MOON

Strawberry month, long after the blood moon, the bleeding orbits in my
father's head,

Spread over us: I was counting fear, dropping the decimal, and starting again
as he slipped and took the stairs like a rocket.

What time is it? he said. What time is it?
he asked until the ambulance came,

And this terrible news reached out for all of us.

Struck with paralysis, I am carried across the plank floor, where the scorpions
loiter, on the wolf-grey night the stars fell as hard as silver spurs.

He smells something like vetiver and orange zest; His chest zings beneath
His light linen robe, printed with pirates with sabres in their mouths.

He smiles at my questions: Are you angry with us . . . sir?

Then smacks the moon from the sky like a piñata and my father and I swipe at it
until a hundred answers, shaped like little animals, are disgorged.

THE CORPSES OF THE FUTURE

My father says, gesturing to the hospital foyer where
the coven of fatsos rolls together for lunch

And a couple of hours of vicious small talk.
I move him forward, past misshapen men with speckled heads,

Past the screaming lady's dark quarters, *Mama!* (is all she ever says),

Past Mr. Ford screaming, Put my leg down! then, Put my leg up! in cadence,

Past the blue room, lit by shadows, where a woman perches on her bed,

Looking out the window, at the brick wall it faces.

We stop at the space at the end of the corridor I call the Disco.

Two white benches meet at the corner by a tall plastic tube filled
with bright, darting fish.

There are buttons to be pressed that make bubbles and foam shoot up;
above is a canopy of dead strobe lights.

The woman in the greasy ponytail joins us and scowls. *Mais je m'assois toujours là,*
she says.

We just keep looking at the chubby green-and-yellow fish.

She's a nice girl, he says, and smiles.

Her mouth makes an upside-down wicket and I stand and wheel my father away,
hissing, You make me sick.

You're sick? My poor little girl, Dad says, his head heavy on his neck,

How flowers list on their stalks, how the music soars then falters in its fright.

The Corpses of the Future, I write in the Mead memo pad: I am taking notes. He asks me to add *force majeure* and *velvet dreams*.

WHIRL

Aristophanes declared chaos to be the new regent, I tell my father, whose eyes roam around, looking for places to light.

These fine, shining knives, or warm pools of still water, have been assailed and his intelligence is now fugitive.

His eyes try to land and miss; his ideas — Could I finesse a plenary indulgence? — are difficult to decode.

There was a shootout today, he says. The crooks were caught, after a hail of gunfire.

He asks me why there is so much evil, happy, in his way, but perplexed.

Whirl is king, I remind him, and he says, Oh, that's right.

All of the tiny salt and pepper packets open into a twister that moves away from my father, and goes looking

For the men in the blood-soaked gowns.

STINKY LITTLE BLANKETS

He rails at the coarse flannels, then kicks them to the ground. He is wearing hospital socks with traction.

Covered in teeth, he says, of the raised white pattern; and a blue-and-white gown, patterned in little squares.

Each square has a caduceus inside: the nurses shed their skin at night and become serpents, or bank robbers, or mafia princesses.

They have taken all of his money and now they want his life.

I had better let you go, they have a knife at my throat, he says one night.
I say goodbye and hang up.

The tip of the knife draws rubies from his skin and mine.

It was never supposed to be this bad.

Don't worry, he would say. I'll always be here for you.

Once, I spent a year not talking to him.

I breathe the last line of the letter he finally sent me:

Come back.

WHAT THE DOCTORS DID

My father was moved from the hospital to the Solomon House and partnered with
an elegant Chinese man who, every night at nine,

Retired to the corner to urinate on the floor.

He was torn; he didn't want to wait until spring for an MRI,
but he was suffering: regardless, they discharged him.

The pain got worse, and after a while he couldn't get out of bed.

The ambulance lit up the boxwood trees as they carried him through the snow.

At the hospital, they discovered his brain had been bleeding the whole time.

They bored holes into his skull as my mother waited in the hallway.

She was the first to see him, his teeth gone, his head bald and held together by a
vee of metal staples.

He looked but couldn't see her.

PT BLIND, the handwritten sign over his bed says.

As soon as the gas wore off, he started screaming.

THE CLOWNS

Are at the hospital every week: their signed photographs are taped in the nurses' station beside a chart of the many faces of feces.

The clowns make dragons from balloons and pull coloured scarves from the mouths of barely sentient patients in wheelchairs;

I am still talking to him when a dove flies in and lands on his arm.

I hear him speaking quietly to the bird; he says, Heather, can we bring it home?

My mother says she doesn't think so,

Then there is a scuffle: the girl clown has grabbed the bird, *Oiseau de merde!*

There is a smaller sound, almost unintelligible,

Another string of my father's heart snapping, the ejection of another pear-shaped tear.

OUTLAW

On his dinner sheet, below *les haricots verts* is a list of utensils.

NO KNIFE, it says.

He has code-whited five times, Incredible Hulking his way through every loose object in the room;

Hurling water and juice at nurses and patients, swearing a blue streak.
Your father is quite vulgar, the sepulchral head of geriatrics tells me.

He has bounced on other patients' beds and chewed his way through each restraint; everyone is mystified, why, I can't say.

He just wants to leave.

He can't see a newspaper or the TV; in one of the many *vigies* he's been thrown out of, they tried to make him cook muffins, and paint.

I'm fucking blind, he said.

Lately, his anger has grown legs.

I will call him and talk about the weather and he'll say, That's nice. Boring, but nice.

One of his full-out rages was directed at my mother and brother.
Maddened by their frequent references to what they had to buy,

He asked that he be buried under a mall so they could visit him when they WENT SHOPPING, legs and arms pumping,

His face mottled: my father's face — as familiar to me as the sky, how the sky darkens so quickly and throws bolts of lightning, booms its deep displeasure,

Then timidly proffers the sun. I'm sorry, he always says. I'm just so tired.

One of the better nurses flirts in a brisk way, brushes off his bad moods and says she still likes him.

One of the beams of light, I mean, blesses him.

THE BRUISE

Poor Dad, my mother writes in the subject box, and attaches a picture of my father, wild-eyed and battered.

He keeps greeting her with new bruises; one day, he is discovered sleeping on the floor and he tells me they have left him on Sherbrooke Street.

He manages to call me. Could I come and get him?
I say no.

I say no to my father, who once carried me on his broad shoulders,
as if I am saying,

Let people walk over you like you are garbage: I don't care.

I'll let you go, he says before hanging up, although he never has.

Dad, you are a fir tree forest in Michoacán, where the monarchs
fly to at the end of the summer.

In fall, they fill the coves, sometimes lifting off

In a gaudy, moving mass of colour,

Then rest again, contented that you are steadfast,
that you are here.

WHERE WE ARE

Seven moves from November to July — this time it's Lachine, a locked ward,

Where Monsieur Charles Paquette screams, HOOOOO, at one-minute intervals,

And a dapper little man blows me kisses as he tries the hot and cold faucets in the small washroom.

Where a black man with lambent eyes stands by the entrance staring with gentle resignation,

Like someone beaten to his sweet pulp.

The mean lady I call Punchy leads two ancient women down the halls like a gang: one reaches into her pants and says gravely, My cunt.

My father sleeps and worries his scarred head.

I look at a family crowded on a faraway balcony and I am in Lachine, at seventeen, on the back of a Harley Sportster, eating up the grid,

My long red hair a signal — I am watching Rob peel his T-shirt off, revealing the colours

That stain his biceps, Mount Sanqing in the blue light of his bedroom.

I see in my mouth a sultry assent, his golden hair falling over the ending.

The ending where I reject him and leave, certain that we will always be beautiful —

Dad, you press 5683 then *,

And just past the elevator is the little garden where the skeletal man smokes, and past that, the whole enchilada.

HEAVEN AND HELL

I pull down the bars and sit on the bed with my father.
Where are we going? he asks. After. To Hell?

Purgatory, I say. We decide it must be like a government office where number seven
is being called and you have a million six.

He remembers different old friends. They are always magnificent.

Very few come to see him; after a while, fewer still.
People don't know what to say, people forget his legendary generosity.

It's hard work and people are very busy, people are insects, industriously
making nests from bits of paper they vomit and spread like paste.

Still, were the room filled with their sounds, he would smile his new,
sightless smile and try to gather them in his hands,

His hands as broad as the Heaven I promise him he is headed to.
Oh God, I hope so, he says. He misses his mother and father.

Two years later, we talk at lunch and he is so happy: Lynn, I died, he says.
I'll see you soon! Are you happy?

I say that I am.

Ecstatic? he says, and I falter.

Say you're ecstatic, he says, and I say I will be, when I get there.

You take your time, he says. Everyone here can't wait for you to sing, though.
As though I am good, I exhale a few notes, as his dad, my kind, quiet grandfather —

My dad woke me to tell me about his death when I was a kid and I said nothing because his frailty scared me; when his mother died ten years later, he said, I'm an orphan now, and my silence stayed stuck, choking us both

— is swaying from a tall ladder as he writes WELCOME in wobbly gilt letters that hang from the clouds.

THE LOBSTER TRAP

During the year before his accident, my father started collecting,
going so far as to work for the Victorian Order of Nurses:

He took pictures of people with their purchases,
selected what books he thought might be valuable.

He wanted to work with me; to sell them online —

Then he branched out: heavy gold-plated necklaces for my mother;

A wiry full-length fur coat, a porcelain doll that plays
the theme from *Love Story*.

Then the paintings: shag rug stapled to canvases making blunt pastorals;
milkmaids and rosy-faced children in baroque frames —

Soon, he started buying without any discrimination. A set of four-foot schooners;
a concrete pig in a dress, cigar boxes.

An old lobster trap, quite intricate and beautiful.

You see, you are just swimming along until something flares or shimmers.

You follow and the trap door snaps shut.

My father was violent today, and the thick strap, with the pins and black oxide
grommets, was tied to his waist.

He is just lying there, aloft and banded.

No longer my worried, chick-fuzz-headed father with his starry plans and
garish love:

On these days, he is a current of rage and sorrow I fall into, sick with wanting,
and drown.

THE RED BLANKET

Belongs to my father; it is a plush square with black whipstitches

That suns itself on his chair back

Where he likes to sit and watch TV with the volume up: anything,
from women's golf to the music of Persia.

He reclines and tosses a small crinkled ball at Samson, the grey cat he rescued
and teaches tricks to,

The cat he lays out damp towels for, who eats from china saucers.

The last time he came to see me, he said that Samson would be mad at him for
leaving, and he was.

It took two days for him to shake it off, and start playing whirling-chair and
sock-stalk again.

The cat I loathe and accuse of tripping him on the stairs in the first place.

He follows me everywhere, anyway.

And catches me, in the middle of the night —

Walking past, I look down and he is rolling and rolling on an old rag rug.

Painfully, I get on my knees and hold him.

I miss him too, I say, and Samson opens his mouth; he opens his orange eyes,
great orange jewels, and cries in anger and pain:

Razing our enemies, beating back the vast, plucking force that seized him, his only friend —

All around lay the inert bodies of beanbag mice and crocheted sardines.

All around the battlefield like numerals fallen before an incalculable loss.

WHAT WOULD YOU DO

If, *when* Dad gets better? I ask my mother on the last night I am there,
then fall asleep.

I see my pillow expand and rest beneath my father's head; watch it wrench open
and snow over us both until there is no pain.

I want to give you this gift, I say, and he thanks me, as we grasp the air
like newborns, at all of its harmless magic and forgetting.

When Dad gets better, I would make us coffee, my mother says, then sit
with him in bed, talking all night.

Her dream reminds me of an incubator I saw for newborn sea horses, so few of
whom survive,

Those golden, constant lovers —

I latch them to my heart, and nourish them: so much rests on their tiny shoulders.

Still, they prevail, in their resolute, ill-starred way.

ARROWS

When you are stabbed, you have to leave the blade inside you.

Suddenly, your body will not know how to live without it.

I don't want to talk to her!
I don't like her anymore, why is everything so much better when she leaves?

My blind father says when I stop talking.

His violence is escalating: I read that I should listen for what he is trying to communicate, is it fear or misery? Actual pain.

His shoulder was dislocated; a disc in his back slipped, before the accident.

They give him a quarter Tylenol, four times a day, an amount that seems, to me, like the protocol for medicating a spider.

One day, he was screaming so loudly, I slipped him half a Percocet. I had seen his spine move like a car on a roller coaster.

Who was that nice nurse? he said. My God, I feel fantastic.

Shut up with that shit, he says one day, when I tell him I love him.

It is not about me, I know. And it is: I have failed him.

When I got to the hospital last time, he wasn't in his room.
He had heard my voice,

And was in the hall in a wheelchair, crashing it into the wall.

My baby! he cried, maddened by his inability to get to me.

I am gathering up this memory like the fleece-covered bones of a lamb,

A lamb that slipped under a fence and was running for its life
before I caught it, and felt in its fear a fatal yearning.

Dad came to my house some summers ago, and insisted on building me
a bookshelf.

He got one, an ugly faux-mahogany disaster, at IKEA, and a can of red paint,
and we spent six hours slamming it together on the patio he drenched in red.

Then we dragged it back in, and he hammered it into some kind of shape,
hoisted it up, and forced it into a gap in the wall.

The paint didn't take: it just pooled in the dented areas like a crime scene.

Jesus Christ, it's like working with a T. Rex, I said, angrily.

We drank wine from a bottle I opened with a screwdriver, and I felt relieved
when he left, and in the morning I laughed

When I saw he had placed a model of the very dinosaur on top of the shelf —

Oh no, it just got real again, a guy on TV said tonight, and cried.

My father would come back that night after a fight with another of us, put away
his bag of toiletries and lie on the sofa.

As I watched him try to sleep, the moon muscled in and flexed, shining on
two still tears on his face.

I kissed his massive head, the lonely man I love the most, always scavenging,
so recklessly, for love.

EXIT STRATEGIES

Six or seven years ago, my father started running away from home.

He would come to my house, with a small suitcase, and say something about *your mother.*

He would get up at dawn, shave, and drive around the city buying large amounts of mulch and soil and bag after bag of Dollarama items — orange plastic sunflowers,

Clothespins, trellises, colourful pails.

I brought him to school with me, and he sat in the very back.
Kids, I said. You had better not fucking embarrass me.

We chipped away at the barren yard, ate pizza, and soon enough he would say,
You know, it's weird, but I miss her.

I knew that this meant he would be gone by morning.

They were kids themselves when they met: in old pictures, they are a little too beautiful, too radiant to look at,

Their secret in plain sight.

Unlike the classified contents of the letter from the Superior Court I received this morning.

I picked it up and it leaped from the envelope and cut my hand to ribbons:

CONSIDERING that it appears from the evidence for the record that the person in question has become incapable of caring for himself or administering his property —

My blood runs in straight lines towards this estimation, and I remember my father, a week ago, confiding in me, They are stealing my money.

My father, who has always worked with numbers like the brush strokes of *Wheatfield with Crows*; that is, beautifully, portentously.

I ask my mother when his phone is coming and she says he's not allowed to have one here,

Here, where he is pinioned nightly, wondering if his wallet is safe in the drawer, hearing cars ignite below his window.

RECORD his incapacity to care for himself, the letter insists.

I jam it back into the envelope and decant today's conversation:

I feel her here, he said. My mother, the perfume she wore, he told me, this long and piercing day: *Bellodgia.*

I have a tiny bottle of this fragrance I keep open to release her, the warrior angel; to smash and return to the court, inside the envelope, with a note:

"Cut your own filthy hands on this and let them bleed."

THE BIRD LADY

My father was on his way to work and swerved to avoid the thing,
then got out of his car.

He brought the hopping sparrow home and we put it in a birdcage,
watched it stare malevolently at the dishes of water and peanuts.

It prevailed and my brother brought it to the Bird Lady, a tough,
snappish woman whose yard was an aviary:

Ostriches speeding after hummingbirds, cardinals hiding from
hawks in the mouths of red tulips.

She plucked the bird from him, sharply twisted its wing and it flew away.

Oh the poor little creatures, my father sometimes despairs, as the sparrow
jumps from its bamboo perch and pecks at his hand,

And, locating a window left open, they valiantly tighten
their bandages and are gone.

A student reads a poem about the birth of her baby.
She is reading it the day I found out my father's illness is fatal.

The poem's intuition suffocates me —

I have never once thought of how scared and lonely the nights must be,

Of how brave he has always been for us.

The poem is called "The Dark Corridor"; in it, the baby longs
for her mother and the mother longs back.

She is reading it on my father's seventy-seventh birthday; in Montreal, my mother
and James, my brother, are buying candles and streamers,

A bucket of chicken, a few sensible gifts, the same as Christmas

When we spent the day with him in the hospital.

Where he opened big, tacky slippers and pyjama pants,
and told the nurse she looked like Gina Lollobrigida,

C'est un compliment.

We took turns holding his hand,
his big, wounded hand that always squeezes back.

Another student reads a poem about his grandson.

I wish I had grandchildren, I guess, my father said, but only once,

And my heart screamed, Let me out!

As my mind coolly turned over this information:
You almost did.

OH, STAY —

We don't talk about God anymore although
Christ was all he could talk about for the first few months.

He often mentions their long conversations in the step-down unit,
he wants to organize what he calls a Pray-down,

A lively revival meeting in a barn. The thought of it makes him smile;
makes us laugh outright, when he starts ad libbing songs.

I feel like a flea in a mattress filled with white feathers, he says;
he apologizes to all of us often, and we will remember these months as

Filled with tears and remonstrations.

There's nothing to apologize for, Dad.

I put a cross around his neck in the violent ward and he throws it across the room.
At home, the frightening cross of his youth springs from my bookshelf,

Ejecting the gold sucker like a piece of toast.
Where has He gone?

I have an awful vision of Him holding His white robes aloft and covering His face,

Dodging the smells, the touch of greedy, witless hands.

When my father dreams, he dreams of robbers
side by side, at large in there,

And awakes, still trembling:

Those are my best days, when I shake with fear.

MODESTINE

We have each tried to read to him, with no success, except for James, who read him
all of Robert Louis Stevenson's *Travels with a Donkey in the Cévennes.*

I was there, in the first of the long-term care centres, when he finished the story,
and we all shared the narrator's sadness about giving up his donkey,

Not having realized that he loved her; unable to retrieve her,
I was lying beside him, listening to the sounds of small, solid hooves and

A tin bell, my father's good breathing,

The kinds of sounds that strike like hammers, later on in life.
He was better then: my phone reminder CALL DAD still appears each night at

Eight, but there are no phones where he is now, no nurses to plead with to let me
speak to him, and anyways, he will have been asleep for hours.

We talked every night for months, then less and now

I wait until my mother, sister, or brother are there, and have short, stilted
talks that end either in tears or in furious impatience.

He has stopped talking about his cat, or his own bed,
and asks some questions over and over, while swerving in and out of sense.

The donkey's feelings are not evoked in the book;

The author also thrashed the abused creature, and God only knows

How she fared with her new owner: inside of her is the baby she was,

Learning to stand, then endure, enduring all.

Please let me go home? my father said out of the blue, not too long ago.

I'll be quiet; I won't bother anyone.

Please, he said again, but so quietly, having been beaten down,

Having seen nothing but the dark, interminable, road ahead

Diminish into a short path, governed by certainties that fly right past him,

By grace itself, by its absence and outrage.

TERMINAL

The downward turn is fast and steep.

Give me a phrase, I asked him today, something for a poem.

Sleep sheableen, he said, thickly, then spelled it several times before dropping the phone.

It has been ten months.

Last winter, before the leeches and the poison,
he and I talked every night and his delusions were rare, two-day

Nightmares, now there are rabbits in the room,

Men with measuring tape and lottery tickets, needles, and pills
forced down his throat.

He rarely cries anymore; has stopped praying fervently;
worse, he rarely laughs or says anything to add to my long list,

Like the day he asked if I lived on a turtle farm,

When he described his lunch as pills and warm water, something
I failed to appreciate at the time.

We cannot hang up pictures or leave him things:
he manages to escape the restraints and tear everything apart.

The good days arrive out of nowhere: today, he says,
I love you, my little girl.

My eyes swell shut.

Two days after his surgery, my brother and I went to see him. He hung his head in
the inexplicable shame that has chased him ever since.

And asked how old he was, and where he was;
how old was I, he asked, and when I told him, he cried so loudly,

Incredulous — What happened? Where did all the time go?
he would soon start calling strangers and old friends to say

He was at Grand Central, could someone come and get him? Jimmy, I'm at the fucking station.

Everyone said no as he stood on the platform hearing that mournful whistle
that is the sound of remembering, departures. Privation.

Just past the rolling boxcars, deep in the woods is the shebeen
where my shanty Irish father drinks moonshine.

Amidst the scorched grass and frail trees is the jewel, his rough mind refined into diamonds.

ENTR'ACTE, A SMALL, DISTRESSED HAIRBRUSH

The lock-code is the same, the cast as well,
returning to Lachine from the Douglas at the end of August,

The worst of the fevers have spiked — my mother's family's injuries,
my mother's penury;

The adjustment to the *hébergement*'s secured floor
where a wiry woman with a full, springy beard keeps taking

My hand and walking me up and down the hall when Dad is sleeping,
past the almost-horizontal woman shaped like a starfish;

The man with the jutting chin and face covered with hard, pale
cysts I have, unkindly, nicknamed Popeye Boil.

My swains, who line up in the kitchenette and Yoo-hoo!
when I pass; Punchy, the woman whose hands are always balled into fists;

And the physiotherapist: a complete grotesque, who has given up on
my father, Who don't see well, *et je ne peux pas marcher avec* lui.

My father, waking from a dream about his platoon and his labours,
says nothing when George, my sunken-faced new paramour,

Walks into his room, rips a waxy orange blossom from the plant on the
window and tenders it to me.

What's happening? Dad finally says as my brother, graciously, tries to guide
George from the room.

This is George, I say.

Get the hell out of here, George, Dad says.

He's a human being, my brother says, deserving of dignity —

Shoot him! my father yells.

And Jim guides him, a bit more firmly, out the door.

I hand my father his toothbrush, and a cup; we tidy his bed, and he asks for
his hairbrush, a light wooden one with soft bristles I bought thirty years ago

That he took from my bureau and put on his own.

He had never wanted anything of mine, things mean very little to him
and I surrendered it happily.

My father's hair is thin and downy; his scalp almost too soft to feel, if a bit
changed from the raised scars.

Mange la merde, maudite vache, Popeye tells the new
préposé, and he is louder than heavy metal.

The light wanes on the plushy bristles moving slowly through Dad's
grey-and-brown hair,

On his now-tranquil face and me, taking notes:

Dad's hilarious thing with the flowers.

I have flicked the bloom into my suitcase: beauty may be something one retrieves
from garbage, but it is this precise company that isolates it,

Aggressing until it shines:

My father's nimbus of thriving, immoderate hair and sweet, faraway theft.

Even George and his memories of other summers; Popeye's *rage raisonnable*.

SLÀINTE MHATH

For David McAskill

The visits have taken on an orderliness that I imagine prison is like, odious and conciliatory in its steadfast regimen.

What must it be like for him, his mind attacked like a painting altered with swipes of turpentine, then left exposed.

There are the fields of his childhood, alive with tiny raspberries, sharp sticks and slowpoke turtles, bleeding into his hoodlum teens.

Did you actually rock around the whole clock, I ask him, when my sister suggests we play his fifties record.

We rocked until the girls said they had to go, or we were too drunk, he says, and remembers vomiting at a party, spills of yellow and green.

A through line of parties with David, his partner in crimes, who visits this August with a stack of bitter chocolate, and stories my father sits up and shares

Of a detested colleague whose plant Dave sprayed every morning with DDT until the man wrenched the tended-to, maddening thing into the trash, spiking the
     earth with

A pencil that Dave began treating with paint remover: Nothing can grow in this! the man despaired,

An open can of sardines left in a heating duct during another colleague's vacation; hours billed to big steaks and tall beers:

He signs his letters with the Gaelic words for Cheers.

One day later, my father forgets that we were there, but he is desperate, the *heavy bear* howls for the bars of chocolate.

He doesn't remember seeing me, but he never forgets who I am,
the most besieged of his platoon, and the most enduring: You're just like me,

He says, and my brother holds his head with infinite tenderness and shaves him,
and I lead him back to bed, in my mind I am lifting him again and he is holding on —

Like Anchises as we stagger through the burning city.

In the very centre of the painting we are untouched by ruin: we are five, furious
and suffering and madly in love.

LABOUR DAY WEEKEND, 2014

Is another long, miserable affair.

On the phone with a young, unemployed friend, I tell her how one of my exes
bought acres of land for next to nothing in a small town.

Good for him, she says.

The Air Show planes keep breaking the sound barrier, as I think of ISIS;
of praying to be happy as James Foley's head falls to the ground,

Again and again

Or the door, starting to move on its spring —

I worry about you are the words that close my only letter,
after I sent a mass email to my university, excoriating them for being

Dullards, and self-congratulatory pests.

After I pick two or three more fights and fall into a half sleep,
dreaming a hotel filled with the sick and preoccupied men of my past.

What happens is

The sun starts to lower its belly, making the air feel like a million stings and
jaundicing everyone;

It illuminates the garbage-filled streets and fat, indolent bodies of those of us not
diving into deep, prodigiously blue lakes,

And then we say goodbye to him, and kiss him.

I always stand in the hall as the door slowly shuts and watch his face
adjust to our absence.

I did everything you asked me, Observant One, he says.
His face lifts like meringue, then collapses and we are gone.

VELAY

It is fall in Velay when Modestine arrives to accept her new burden, white bread, black bread, mutton and bottles,

A pilot coat and more supplies that make her tiny feet tremble.

As fall rushes straight at us, I remember how innocently we believed in the surgeon — who would tell me to stop bothering him, after two messages —

In the teams of nurses and digital images of a traumatized, yet recoverable, brain.

It was late last fall when my father would tell us, every day, that he was feeling much better; that he was ready to come home.

When we talked every night at eight, about taking a long vacation, or building a house.

As the days got longer, his became shorter: sometimes, he stiffens and screams for help in a raw voice I do not know.

Sometimes he is drugged into a catatonia that the nurse blames on his bath, *Comme les petits bébés*, she says, and shrugs.

Each new round of super-drugs brings more fatigue and hunger:

They are loading him with chemical weights and lashing at him to behave himself.

I'm sorry, he sometimes says, hopelessly, or, giving up, he tilts his chair and falls to the ground on his side, tied tightly to its metal bars with rags.

My mother found him that way, and called for help.
Don't you dare leave, I am sure she says at times like this or on

The day he wouldn't wake up

And his eyes were swollen shut with conjunctivitis and his dentures had slipped, making him look like an old vampire,

Like a joke he would hate; he hates being laughed at. He is afraid of everything he has been entrusted with; he is afraid.

My sister has written beneath a crayon drawing of our father: his eyes are X'd shut; his face looks mild, and apprehensive.

Et son épaule droite fait très mal! she writes on the adjacent drawing, adding red and orange pain-rays to his arm.

Today he tells me he is tired of living this way, and wants to die.

Who will I talk to? I think, and we cry and carry on, as we so often do, because everything is ruined.

I went quickly outside and tried on jackets that looked like monkey-furs, and one that looked like a toy monkey's fuzz,

Thinking I can't afford this, or anything, until I found myself wobbling down the street, holding, at one point, a small bag of oranges that my hand released:

O the little suns sliding down slicks of dark rainwater!

It won't be too much longer, I think, hurrying home now, where the pills and knives and poisons are

Some faint, still powerful memories, of love and mercy.

A GOOD DAY

After I have written a series of job applications, beginning *Help me, for the love of God*, I get a call from my mom.

She is outside with Dad, in the garden that forms a circular mass beside the centre.

He sounds happy; happier when I remind him that they are close to the little store where a volunteer sells ice cream bars and soda.

Heather, let's go to the Tuck Shop! he yells, and we say goodbye:
my heart lifts like smoke and spreads.

I go to the Dollarama and buy sixteen little lanterns for the stairs,
a tub of cotton candy, small envelopes and poster paint — things from the lists

I make every night and rarely check.

Is that good? I ask a woman at the cash buying water flavourer; Let me help you, I say to another, and, showily, open the door.

I just want to talk to someone

And say, What if my dad gets better and everyone was wrong?

What if he grabs his jacket and hat, and breaks through the door with guile or a brick?

What if he calls a taxi, and comes home and sits in his chair, reclines, and coaxes his angry cat to play with the small red ball?

It is like being inside a wall of water, the sheet of tears I see through, seeing you, Dad, safe and returned home.

Sometimes, my mother will drop me off at Le Topaze, a strip-mall bar sparsely filled with sad old bastards in sports jerseys and cargo shorts.

As she shops for dinner, I play whatever songs I can find among the mystifying array, like "Hellraiser," or "Big Poppa."

I ask Jerry, who is sitting beside me and making small, nauseous gestures with a damp napkin, what he would like to hear; ask Doris, the waitress, for change, which

She will get, When I'm damn good and ready!

I knuckle C-28, and play Plastic Bertrand for him and Jimi Hendrix for Doris, who makes a nice little grunt as she slams my beer down.

Jerry is going to visit his brother in Burlington, and is visibly excited: he itemizes the contents of his suitcase, and shows me pictures of the guest room in the
    basement,

A single bed, an end table and a framed picture of his brother gutting a deer.

They sent me this and said I could stay as long as I liked, he says, flushed with pride and the shock of the quadruple bypass he is recovering from.

And we clink bottles as my poor mother stands at the door, resigned: she is used to this, resigned to hearing me, a little drunk, recite Rocky's speech to his loser kid,

You or me or nobody is gonna hit as hard as life!

I thought your father was good today, she will say, as she cleans leaves of venous red lettuce and leaky, oblong tomatoes.

Remember how he put all the hazelnuts on his chest, and he knew how many were there?

Later in the night, I imagine, the Topaze is filling up — its tables, its bar and dance floor — and as my mother and I try to sleep, they lean into each other, imprecating,

Linger on, your pale blue eyes,

Which makes my eyes water until I consider that my father's eyes are topaz-coloured, and as acute as scalpels;

That he too is trying to sleep, by reckoning where all the crackers, cookies and chocolates are, and counting how many are left, and calibrating the moon's slant

Towards early morning's reconnaissance mission, at dawn, when the sky reveals itself to him as his likeness, cut into sharp, brilliant bars.

One of the new staff members, an educator, asks what books our father might like, and my brother says eighteenth-century picaresque novels, with painterly scenes,

And books about monsters.

One day, we all went to Niagara Falls, and I dragged my parents to the tacky side: they were used to Niagara-on-the-Lake's restaurants and the Christmas-tree ornament store.

My dad and I had our pictures taken as magazine covers: he was the grisly biker on *Easyriders*; I was the mutant-headed Cosmo-girl.

We went to the House of Frankenstein, a green mansion south of a mammoth sculpture of the creature itself, eating a BK hamburger.

Inside, it is instantly pitch-black and unstable: hands reach out from the walls and grab or pinch; high, menacing voices urge us to leave.

But we are running on rolling bars and can't find the way out — so I start screaming just as another girl does.

Her boyfriend is appalled and scolds her: You wanted to come in here, get it together!

Dad, I call, finding the hem of his T-shirt; Dad? the scared girl mews, snatching up the other end,

And, without comment, he leads us both past the grabbers and screamers, over the rolling barrels, and into the sun.

As I write this, I apprehend some of his darkness, and am ashamed that this story has always been about me.

About me and that girl, clinging to my fearless father,
who means it when he says that he wants to get out.

You're sounding better every day, I said yesterday, and he said, What was I like before?

Nice, I said. The same, I thought — *Facta non Verba* practically carved on your chest.

LION

In September, the ball of gas seems to lower in the sky, grazing us with its fat belly, signalling its regrets.

The sun is my father's star.

As it diminishes this year, he too moves farther away.

So we are burned, in part, by his small, stubborn request to go home; so we shake, before the prospect of the shorter, colder days.

His neighbour writes me this morning: I miss my friend.

He tells me about driving with him to thrift stores to find things for all of us, to leave to us.

He says that my dad told him that he and I were alike, in many ways.

All day, I berate myself for not having gone driving with him instead, as squirrels scrabble in the soffits of the decayed roof.

As my old dog struggles to keep up on our walk.

As I blow my stack when the cat shits by her water bowl, roar like a lion and retreat to my room.

I remember that, as I walked, I told myself, slowly, as if learning how to speak, that the sun is on my shoulders;

Right now the sun is on my shoulders and everyone is still alive.

AND THEN, IN SEPTEMBER

Somewhere between the kitchen and living room, his heart stopped.
My father died, my mother said, and we breathed in each other's shock.

Between viewings and the service, my distraught father: Why can't I come to the
funeral?

Then further mourning, for my mother's sisters, killed in their teens, and this small
resolve: They were spared this inglorious sojourn, he says,

Tears racking his face.

Dad is changing fast in intervals: he wrests his bed from its stanchions and pushes
it to the middle of the room, where he is sailing.

Asks who the monkey is in the picture I have drawn of him and will only eat the
all-dressed hot dog that Jimmy gets him with pinking-sheared fries.

I don't think I'm going to make it, he says, more often.

I have taken down all of his room and phone numbers from the side of my bureau;
there is no way to reach him.

Replaced them with photographs of me and him, and our same-smiles,
and one shot I don't remember taking,

Of him sitting in a little chair in the yard, alone.

It is shot from the back and he is nested between his pots of morning glories,
oddly frail and defenceless,

As though the blows are gathering force, just off-camera; as though he hears their
evil intentions and is struck.

I can still smell the Montreal metro; hear its hushed zip and the cry for the end of the line.

Il devient plus difficile, chaque fois,

To look at my notes and plump them into these words; to evoke you, bruised and furious,

Or lost and alone at the place we grew up thinking of as a dirty mental institution, at the dirty mental institution where you have a bed and that's all,

Where I was able to reach you and you said you were sitting at the dining room table, tired, but not allowed to sleep —

I worry you have done something wrong and are in trouble.

The doctors, fed up and helpless, want to suction out your testosterone; want to keep taking more and more of who you are, and tossing it

Like latex gloves and gory instruments.

He gets angry and screams, the nurse who let me speak to him says, and I say, *Naturellement,* and *Merci, merci bien.*

Someone has stolen his clothes: when my sister visited him the other day, He was wearing something indescribable, like a onesie?

And no one even pretends they might visit anymore.

And so we five shudder in a soaking nest on a skinny branch: it is all we can do, we brush against and feed him; we stay awake, making noises

That tell the predators that we have prevailed   sopping

        scrawny things

bright-eyed with tears

              & sharp of claw if

Beat-up, half-broken & never I mean rarely hopeful of rising with the sun.

My father is the funniest man I know, which is hard on him.
When we talk, I can sense his mind lying in wait, for the joke he can sign off on,

So I will still be laughing when he, abruptly, says goodbye, in accordance with the
scripture of true humour, which insists an audience be left wanting.

After a week of quiet misery, with a new collection of ward-mates my enervated
brother has named, in part, Larry the Mop, Dooris, Billy Goat and Norm,

Dad is light on the phone, absorbed in a drawing project with my mother.

I'm drawing a tree, he says.

I ask him to add Frankie, and he says, OK, here are his ears, and — I think,
a big smile.

That sounds nice, I say, happy for whatever he can see. Did you draw his collar?

My mom has her cellphone on speaker: He is going to draw after you talk;
he's telling you how the tree will look with Frank beside it.

And me?

Long hair, he says, remembering my new weave.

There — a pretty lady, he says, and his voice is as clear as a cold hand passing across
glass.

We were caught up in an unexpected typhoon of happiness: I am going to hang up
now, he says.

So I can have this moment.

And then he and my mother, I imagine, filled a page together, with a forest.

In the forest, they are young and sleeping in a bed of moss, amidst their love and their children and their secret world — buried and marked with an X

On a map that they burn when the sun goes down — it blooms into moonlight:

The moon that, paler now, scratches at my mother's lonely room, and bangs itself against the windowless walls of his cell, and bays.

I wish for you to hold the moment, to stuff in it the one thing you still have from home, your own soft pillow that you carry everywhere,

I wish the pillow filled with lush sighs, brave dreams
and flight feathers

Barbed with hope, with still more downy, red-pigmented instances
of inestimable value.

FOR THE HAT TRICK

Two days, Dad.
I spoke with your temporary doctor; my doctor called her too.

She agreed to adopt a new, holistic view; to stray from the firmly pharmacological
resolution:

Suddenly, a walking-schedule appeared on his wall; the shiftless CNIB staff
called to make an appointment.

And you sounded so clear. Before I knew it, I was telling you a long, tricky story
about publishing; about the villains and one or two heroes —

You were right there.

I let myself hope again, in spite of Christmas coming, when your simple wish —
to sit at a table with all of us — will not come true.

Conjure the wrenching tension and outright violence into a bubble,
a sweet bubble, jasmine or eucalyptus, which may have emerged from your big tub,

The one you would call me from and pretend you were in the living room until a
telltale *splish* gave you away.

One of your rare baby pictures features you lying on your stomach at three or four
years old, stark naked, reading a book.

You are modest but aggravated by clothes; a shy loudmouth and an aloof,
lovestruck father,

Why does none of this matter?

My former GP told me she had zero curiosity about her training cadaver,
when I pressed her.

Dying to tell me the truth: We couldn't do our jobs if we actually cared!

But today—

My brother's nicknames are simple enough. Billy Goat eats tin cans; Dooris is forever lingering at Dad's door singing,

Mais il m'a coupé la langue—

Larry the Mop lies on the floor all day; Norm is exceedingly normal, often chiding other patients for their actions: Stop polishing the table. It's clean, let it be.

Today, I struggle to hear you over the din of another lady, who screams like a crow.

There were three of them, my mother tells me later. She tells me about ABC, the lady who shouts the alphabet.

And you were tired, Dad.

Your sister and her husband were visiting, there was all this noise.

And you said, I'm not in a hospital, incredulously, when I talked about getting you home.

But I'll give you a buzz tonight, OK? you said, and I said, Sure. Please do.

I hung up and went back to bed. Woke up at 4 p.m., sick and dirty. Almost done.

It won't be much longer, you said.

As the maenads raved, locked even out of wishing.

Norm finally visited my father's room: my mother perked up. Hello, he said, congenially.

He was wearing a small Alpine sweater and a diaper.

I prayed that if you had three good days, we were finally on our way, even though your other, jaded doctor told me *Qu'il y a rien d'intéressant à propos de cette maladie.*

By interesting, he means corrigible.

Today was going to be the new day. Everything inside me is screaming to be heard, but I won't listen.

My father will come back. Look how close we came this time!

THE DOCTORS, IN PART

My father's doctor, who speaks of his illness as not *interesting*, also has sick parents. His siblings loathe his rational sense of pathosis, he tells me.

He imparts to us an essential truth: the good days come and go, a fine insight that fits into the puzzle I have created,

One that is equal parts suffering and magical certainty.

Dr. Z—— is cold, but empathic. But the affable doctor, the motorcycle-hipster, who operated on and almost killed my father outright, wrote me:

May I kindly request you not write me again. Make sure all of your inquiries go through my secretary, not to this personal email.

I called her and he never returned the call.

He thinks I'm a can of SPAM, I told my mother, morosely, not my father.

But he hadn't hurt my feelings.

I keep his letter, this glacier, in a file labelled WORK, with the collected odiousness of the last year, and concentrate.

The motorcycle MD, the men who pull my father's mangled arm until he cries, the slit-lipped woman who detests him on sight:

I will chase them through Hell for you, Dad.

Before turning them over, like the last of this fall's leaves that break as I gather them, with the worms and the shit and the layer of rough snow;

Bag them, and leave them on the curb with the express request that they never be returned,

That they burn in metal cans that old men abrade their hands over, elementally, having changed something worthless into bright, palliative fire.

SUNDAY

No one came to see you today, Dad.

My mother was late, she says, and you were asleep. It happens and it can't be helped, she tells me, sharply.

I called, after sleeping all day, again.

In my dark room, surrounded by the wretched smell of my anger and *désespoir*.

You cleared your throat as you took the phone, and said hello.

You were distracted.

I'm just in the middle of a bid, you said.

Antiques, or poker, I am not sure which. But you were sleeping,
and my call woke you so you could place the number.

You thank me.

And you say, I'll call you tonight, not knowing that you can't.

Now you curl from the salt of heartbreak by losing yourself harder and
faster,

In the graceful fall of the horses' spurred-on feet

That gets louder and more like the deep keys, how whales vault from deep seas —

And you are standing and waving your straw hat at Black Jack, the clear winner.

This horse has lost everything and he still won't do what he's told, you want to tell
me,

But you are alone at the procession; you are alone as the casket passes slowly by.

THE NIGHT OWLS

My father and I used to make late-night runs to the pharmacy at the Beloeil strip mall,

For Old Port Tipped cigars and paperbacks: we both liked to read late into the night, when I was twelve and he was thirty-eight.

We read indiscriminately: *The Naked Nun, Jaws, Suffer the Children* — we both found the latter so hideous,

So disturbing, my dad said, a word I admired instantly, that we hid it in the garbage in case anyone else read it by mistake, not knowing what we knew,

About the girl and the cave and the smut and depravity: I still can't think of it, unless it is to remember our brave crime.

He has not read anything for over a year now; my sister writes from his room without windows:

> — Dad is in pain — his lower back & right
> shoulder. Dr. F—— said she would get
> him heating pads, but they haven't materialized.
>
> All of his clothing has been purloined.
> Every day he's been put in a polyester unitard.
>
> He was unshaven and had wet socks today.
> He's really sad ☹

Mary, the family's sun, setting in this accidental poem.

Tomorrow he is being returned to Lachine, with some new meds and instructions. We are happy to have him closer to Mom,

Silently prepared for more good days and bad.

Like the night last week when I talked to him before he went to bed.
I said, I'll call you tomorrow.

I'll be here, he said.

Or tonight, when he said, You are a wonderful daughter, and I want to see you so much. But I am going to die.

Please wait for me?

Then, as they do every night, someone hung up the phone for him as I called out, Don't go,

As I guess I did when I was a kid and he almost died in a car crash, and took so long to come home while he was laid up, he learned how to make paper flowers,

And he sent them to me, in paper baskets.

There are Christmas cards on the table for me and my dog and cat, from Mom and *Grandpaw*.

I stay up until sunrise every day, reading owlishly, anything as long as it's junk.

You wait for me! I say out loud,

As if my father is reading upstairs and I can meet him in the kitchen and bury the unspeakable below a corona of eggshell and serrated grapefruit half,

Or he is just gunning the engine as I pull on my plaid jacket and jump into the '64 Impala: it is *an alert and wary animal* that can outrun time.

ELBA

My father asked for peace and quiet for his birthday and for Christmas and Father's Day, every year.

I want to live like Napoleon, he said. Exiled in silence on my Elba.

In their early fifties, my parents moved to Curaçao, one of the ABC islands, just north of Venezuela.

He worked for some Dutchmen there, moving money around, and my mother volunteered at an orphanage.

They went to church every Sunday: one Christmas Eve, my father asked my sister and me to go to the early-morning Mass.

We declined and he offered us money. I'll give you fifty, no, one hundred guilders. Has it come to this? he said.

They stayed for many years, and on our last family visit we sat at the beach and watched the sun go down.

Dad disappeared and I went off to find him.

He was sitting in a rowboat, also watching the sun cannonball into the water, in a great violet splash.

The boat was called the *Elba*, I noticed.

He had put his shoulder to his dreams. Dad, why won't you get better?

In Curaçao, there are hundreds of stray dogs, all of them big yellow curs — fireworks are set off on every holiday,

Huge repeating rockets, poppers, sparklers and shells.

This terrifies the dogs and in the morning you drive the fast streets and keep swerving,

There are so many dead dogs on the road, who ran there, out of their minds with fear, only to be struck,

To be battered and ground into peace, then quiet.

WHERE ARE MY TEETH?

Où sont mes dents? my father — who I have never heard speak French — asks.
He is fluent, it turns out: he and Sofi, the blond orderly, talk and listen to the same

'50s Hits CD: she holds his hand and spins around his chair.

His teeth go missing for two days.

I have his spare set, and send them express in a quilted jewellery box.

These are the ones he had made for him down south, which turned out to be
absurdly tiny, as if he had a necklace of seed pearls in his mouth.

He grew a moustache until he was able to replace them.

Where did you put them, Dad?

I threw them under the railroad tracks.

They turned up with the dirty sheets and towels.

In 1955, Elvis sings, *Train, train,*
About a sixteen-coach monster cornering the rails,

His baby seated inside, looking at everything passing by and bumping
over jagged canines, smashed incisors and molars.

Even if he is in a terrible mood, my father likes to sing, and this day
we harmonize, stamping hard on the *long black train,*

That cold scrounger, *le pirate monstrueux.*

HORTICULTURAL SAVAGE

Is what my father calls Lily, whose gift of roses are returned to me because
she will eat them.

Every day in bright lime green, and beaming: we have all been called here, after he
fell and would not wake up —

His breathing is bad, the nurse said, handing over the keys to the palliative room.

I made it there in a few hours, calling to him, Don't go, don't go, and somewhere in
mid-litany he sat straight up and asked for water.

We arrived on our mother's birthday after all.

She looks wrung out and small as she opens card after card,
holds up her sponge cake after the candles have been iced.

The night I arrive, Jim has to get Mary, and I clamber over the bars of Dad's bed
and lie beside him.

Comme un singe, I later explain to the amused orderly.

I put on Motown hits and we talked as the sky changed from dead blue to
a rush of black,

We talked about little Michael being like an angel on loan and seeing the
Temptations on a sunny day,

And talked until the others came back, and Mary, so relieved, spun like a top and
made up a song called "Papadoo."

I'm with you, Dad, my strong, shaken brother says as he takes our father's hand.

And we planned what we would do the next day, after tucking him under the fuzzy
blankets he likes, with the snowflakes and stars.

We will get him 7UP and a peanut butter sandwich, clean clothes and a board game.

And open the door a little nervously.

Still stuck between our shoulder blades the knife that says, Your father is almost dead —

That holds in the blood of remorse and guilt, the vast stream comprising all the little losings so far and the red ocean to come.

EASTER

Dad can often make out the grid of streets from his window, a slice of the Oratory.

Sometimes he sees my mother on a balcony in just a light sweater, and worries.

Falling golf balls: they are birds, I tell him, and he is embarrassed.
I'm just trying to figure things out, he says.

What and when he sees is a mystery to us: suddenly, the bed screws are buttons
that the cats might choke on;

The restraint on his wheelchair is one of his torturer's devices.

One night, he must have spotted the enormous Laura Secord Easter egg my mom
left on top of his closet.

She came at lunch and, seeing the empty box, asked if it was good.
Yes, he said, and smiled.

At Easter he would hide tiny foil-wrapped eggs everywhere.

For months I would find them in hampers and drawers; once, in the slot
behind the telephone.

I dragged a chair to reach in the cupboard above the fridge and found one there.

This was proof to me of an Easter miracle. My dad can't reach that high,
I told one of my friends.

I slept lightly and could not imagine how the Bunny also managed to hide so many
eggs in our little apartment,

How he reached the top of that closet; how he stood up without help,

How his silken ears twitch, as he remembers the rush of yellow yolk then the
sacred sweetness of the shell.

CROOKS

The spring finally wakes and rolls over into summer: it has been eighteen months.

I am sleeping entire days beside my wheezing dog, who, seeing me, smiles.

Getting him outside, into the heart of the riot of colour and sound,

I choose seeds at the hardware store, the ones that look like they have the best chance to survive,

Weave Frank through the colours and sounds as people's happiness adheres to us like pollen I want to wash away, like the cling of foul humidity.

The defiant sun telling me, with brute malevolence, that I will pay and pay.

It was thieves today, picking at him as he slept, tossing his pockets.

He got up, of course, forgetting he cannot walk, and went down like an oak.

Five people had to lift him using hydraulics.

I hurt my fat ass, he says.

Yesterday, nineteen cats died in a fire.

His misery was absolute.

In 1972, he identified my young aunt's body, with my mother's father. Dead in the Blue Bird fire,

His own, terrible, story.

He relives it often, this, or losing his parents, more grief.

We had fought for a long time before his accident, about nothing and everything that pride musters and burns.

He finally wrote me a letter that ended in a prayer, and I seized it, quickly, from the flames.

FOR THE PERSON SUFFERING

From dementia, it is traumatic to relive certain events over and over. As such, certain topics should be avoided —

This is how I started lying to my father.

I read an article by a Dutch doctor, which instructed me never to say, No, Dad, your mother has died,

To watch his face crumple in confusion and pain.

This spring, when he asked me about our bets on the horse race, I made up names for the runners, and he added Hurry up Honeybun to the list:

One hundred on the nose! he said.

Later I would try to register the name, and get into an awkward, meretricious conversation with a horsey sort located outside Leeds.

Today, tired as ever, I listened carefully to my father's story about the football game.

He was taking me to see the Alouettes versus the Roughriders, but could I call about the tickets?

Of course I can, I said.

I'm on this damn boat, he said, and I told him I would send Mom the information.

They think I have some illness, he said. Expialadocious.

I repeated the word, as though writing it down.

We've never been to a game before, I said, feeling winded from the little smacks to my heart.

I want to take you, he said.

He and I are in a fall stadium, drinking spiked coffee as he explains the rules of football.

We are wearing Als hooded sweaters, and once in a while his arm presses against mine and I double over in pain, reliving the very thought of my father

Wanting to take me to a game.

DISASTER

Your father has been wheeled into the common area, and I can't get at him, my mother says.

Someone left the water on in his room, and the floor is four inches deep.

She tells me he is angry, and to call back.

I practice my French on an app featuring a green owl, my coach, wearing a red headband and a whistle.

Il est en colère et confus.

The nouns are returning to me, *abeille, fraises, chaussettes* —
Lite-Brite pegs, slowly filling the black mass with a field of flowers

That often shake loose, and I am speaking to his nurse and there is only wind gathering force in my head, and pulling away the language.

Lily, who never speaks, has taken to leaving my father presents: a stuffed bear, irregular blankets, small pairs of pants she folds and places in his drawer.

Lily donne des mots à mon père,
a way of saying that she recognizes him, his loneliness and need.

Her eyes are enormous and hazy. As he rails this day, she listens.
My mother will return him to his room and find two knives crossed on the bed

Comme une prière féroce.

THE LOVE LETTERS

The 208 letters, sent between my father and mother in 1961, went missing
after he bound them for her,

Somewhere in the chaotic transit back from the Island to their road trip, in a
midnight-blue Cadillac Seville, through America that ended in Toronto, briefly,

Then Montreal: before Pointe-Claire, there was a posh apartment on Sherbrooke
Street, where a neighbour complained about them ceaselessly.

He is riding motorcycles through the kitchen, the hag would say, snarling through
their one shared wall.

Sometimes my father says he has been assaulted, scaring us.

Could this have happened in his past? I ask my mother, in whose memory whirls
letter after letter folded precisely and signed with love from *Jas.*

Another image, of cutting the envelopes to release all the stories he had about
living one year alone in Toronto and missing her,

Still another, of me looking at, and defiling, them.

The house in the West Island is filled with bright tiles and bowls and pictures: all
over the yard, tiny pine trees grow.

No, my mother tells me firmly.

There were never secrets between us, she says, giving me something rare that I
close my hand over:

The secret of their great love and, with it, where I come from, that they still pass to
each other, hand to hand.

REMEMBRANCER

I know I'm getting old, my father told my mother this week: I can't remember anything at all.

The spring is a marauding crow, landing in its cold shadows to frighten away all the warm colours painted on the pigeons' backs — this was the chill park today,

Where I dragged Frank behind me like a sled, dragged him up the steps of the church to the red doors where I rest or bash my head,

Mumbling my prayer: *I'm all wrung out and I have nothing left.*

Sometimes, the man with the long hair steps onto his balcony and plays "Kashmir," or we see children's shoes spiked to the fence, and leave them be and

I hold Francis high to smell the lavender blossoms and we take a sweet hit.

The clouds in his eyes, his corroded breathing: how long will it be?

As we pick our way home, I think of the woman, my age, who used to walk a very old dog, slowly; her head wrapped in a scarf, her eyes ringed with cancer.

I never see her anymore. Or Lucky, or Piggy, Hoople, Molly, Cosi, or Ransom, I think, remembering my dog's friends.

My father is "terrible" today. Having been viciously beaten by at least six criminals, he is in shock and pain.

This did not happen, but it did: some violence was unleashed on his mind; these are the worst of the blows.

Knowing that something is very wrong and that worse, more viciousness, awaits.

I wrap each day in linen and polish its memories: my good dog, lying on the blanket called Blue Magic,

My anxious father, what his soft head feels like, like cotton growing wild, plucked and pendant as a thought —

Five miles from his house on the Island, this cotton grew in a patch by the Shack, a rest stop that sold cold beer and warm cheese pastachies.

It is a sunny day and I am holding on to it as our bottles sweat and we crash them together,

It is a sunny day and I am with my father, my dog unborn and everything waiting, waiting also to become undone.

SNOWBIRD

As my neighbour yelled at me last night, I barely listened.

Something about life being short enough without him having to worry about whatever it was I had mentioned.

I let the nausea that has become another organ entirely do its flips, and forgot about him: he was right, as brutish people often are.

On the way home from another useless job interview, I see two restaurants named Frank, then an art show called *After Frank*.

I call my father, who cannot hear over the street noise, and he says, I'm so tired, call me later?

The rigid lady on the streetcar beside me leaps up the second she can get away from me: am I talking to myself again?

My hands reach for each other like two saps in a meadow.

I think of my life as a short drink that burns and glows, as I see my street in a new way: as a place I will be leaving.

It's not so bad, just buildings, just a line of trees skirted with white or purple flowers.

Tomorrow, Frank will have his ultrasound, meant to explain his falling over and not eating, at almost fifteen.

At the meeting, we sat in the sun on Bloor Street; one table over, a young woman took out a giant aerosol can and sprayed her entire body with SPF 50.

The man I met told me about Anne Murray's stalker.

We also talked about dementia, which I said was, like poetry, a different, highly symbolic, way of speaking.

The stalker used to live beside him in Saskatchewan.

While he was driving his tractor, a flock of snowbirds appeared and assembled in a circle above him.

One alone — these are precious creatures, with fast streaks of black racing like braces along their puffy white heads and breasts —

Is magical, but a flutter is a sign.

This sign moved the farmer to a kind of madness, although he wasn't wrong.

Every day, God tries to get our attention, as in dreams. He pitches us meaningful curveballs, and listens for the sound of the bat

Making hard contact; for the whoosh of the ball that signals its rising significance: failure or swift advancement;

Often foul errors for example I thought things were getting better.

WHAT WAS ONCE RUSSIA

The CCP or whatever, my father says, anxiously. I've been here for fifteen years.

I remind him that Francis is almost fifteen — his limp little legs unable to get up
the streetcar steps today, *My baby*, I said, lifting him up —

So it can't have been that long.

Summer is shuffling forward: in the park we are glanced by a yellow Frisbee and
green ball and every day

My mother calls with a smaller voice, to tell me something that Dad said.

Did I tell you he wrote a poem? she says and Do you want to hear it?

She tells me:

> *Birds and bees and buffalo weeds.*

And today: Your father said today that he is sitting in front of a big blackboard.
That it is dark and everything is erased. He can't remember anything.

Oh! a young girl cried when I lifted my sick dog.

Oh no, I think, very quickly before the eraser speeds over,
she is telling the days of his dying —

The spongy rectangle leaves something like skywriting's passing,
a faint impression of something crucial in its blown-out clouds.

I'LL BE THERE

My mother calls from the train station: Mary is on her way.

One time, on the long trip from New York, my sister saw a girl sit for seven hours without moving a muscle.

On other trips, she falls asleep on strangers' shoulders, or writes her stories: in a new one, Taylor Swift kick-boxes all the mannequin legs in Lululemon and wins!

The sound of the trains is what lives in all of us, tearing beneath *where there is love.*

My father delights in her: since she was a daffodil-haired baby, she has always pulled joy towards us,

Like the plush blankets she and my father call vuvs.

This morning, they call and have been listening to music.

My father, whose voice sounded stepped-on last night, after having narrowly escaped death by hanging, is ebullient.

He and Mary are yelling, my mother's smaller voice chimes in and they set the CD player to Dad's and my song.

The three of them and, briefly, Sofi — having poked her head in the room — sing "I'll Be There" to me,

So loudly, and with such joy, I feel I have just called their names,

That, honey, I just looked over my shoulder
and they, clamorous bags of spilling sugar, are here.

BREATHE

When you get winded on the ice, you feel like — you'll never get your wind back.
— Joe Bowen

I have made a file of my father's emails. There are so few, leaving aside the ones
he forwarded from clusters of friends,

Jokes, like the Six Best Smart-Ass Answers of 2006, #4 being:

A lady was picking through the frozen turkeys at the grocery store, but
she couldn't find one big enough for her family.
She asked a stock boy, Do these turkeys get any bigger?
The stock boy replied, No, ma'am, they're dead.

I told him this joke yesterday, and he said that
he wanted to sleep, his voice rising with impatience.

He is always anxious to hang up now; my mother keeps the phone on speaker and
sometimes modifies what he says, if he seems too abrupt or uncaring:

He is smiling, she said, about the dead bird joke.

Lately I have been pretending that an elderly movie star is my boyfriend.

I need his beefy suntanned arm around my shoulder; to bury my tear-fattened face
in his neatly combed cotton-top.

There, there, he says on the saddest of days, fully posh with a splash of Scouse,

We'll none of this.

My boyfriend will drive me to Montreal, *no questions asked*, in a silver Mercedes
with "Ode to Joy" rolling down the windows.

Tell me about your father, he says, frowning at the maple frosting on his Timbit.

I stuff three in my mouth and sound like Don Corleone when I say, He's very funny. He told us this joke when we were kids, called Bad Man José.

As we pass the Motel des Érables, _____ gets me to tell the whole joke, which is long and crudely accented.

Quite good, he says, smiling patiently and whisking crumbs from his lilac-coloured polo shirt.

Years ago, I found a picture of a restaurant called BAD MAN JOSÉ'S.

I sent it to my father with the caption, WE HAD DEENER TOGETHER, which is the joke's punchline.

He never mentioned it, as if to say, I'm so over it.

When his voice starts to climb, I am scared he is over me as well.

But he always says I love you before hanging up, and he always has.

A good man, my boyfriend says, then dissolves, returning to his villa in Ojai, to the warmth of the pool,

The pool in the middle of the park, not the high, hard monkey bars,

The ones I fell from at four, flat on my back at my father's feet, winded.

Years later he told me he had never been more afraid.

Still and white, I lay on my back until the wind, not all of it and not ever again, came back.

AN HEIR AND A SPARE

On Father's Day, my mother called from my brother's phone and started handing him my presents.

That's heavy, he said, and, I can't see that.

The phone wasn't on speaker: no one could hear me calling his name.

My dog's ears turned pure grey this week.

He couldn't make the long trip, and I couldn't leave him.

Later, I get a picture of Dad, buttoned into the aloha shirt I bought him, which is obviously too tight, but he is smiling, wearing the cop glasses I sent as well.

Then everyone converges at my grandparents' house for their first June without Poppy, and plants rose bushes and cleomes.

My nervous illness is raging by Monday, and Dad's teeth are gone again.

I have an extra set, he says.

But I told the waitress I'd give twenty-five dollars to whoever found them. I found them myself, and I want you to have the money.

I thank him and he asks if he can leave.

I think you have to stay, I tell him, and he says, Oh, OK, quickly, as he steps on his disappointment and misery;

His growing understanding that he needs us, and that we are useless.

After everything he has done for me!

I am just sitting here, writing about him; he is just facing a wall he can't see, trying to figure out how to mail me money if his wallet is gone,

While everyone keeps saying it's not.

Your father had a good day, my mother says.

He had ribs and lemon pie.

In the picture my brother sends, he is beaming.
In June 1967, he became the father of a son.

Sonny, he calls him, the odd time, and James, his own middle name,
when their talks become dense and freighted.

When he was little, I dressed him after his bath, in white terry
karate pyjamas, and my parents and their friends shouted,

It's Cary Grant!

My father held his soap-sweet dumpling tight —

This one is from me, I heard my brother say: one Misty Shell pea lying
companionably beside the other in a *measure of mutual support.*

I might tell you how I had a teenager sit for Frank, who had a boy over and left sexy remnants on the bed.

That Frank hurt his paw somehow and pulled out, from deep in a bin, his detective dog toy.

Look around, he was telling me, Dad, like the time you came here and lost your temper and stormed off, and he scrounged for what you had given him:

A bright yellow sun with orange rays that he dropped sadly at my feet.

We would wonder at my dog's weird intelligence and you would be mad that the teenager let him get hurt and I would also ask you,

Did you cry last night? Because I was turned on my side, feeling kicked in the belly; I mean, worse than usual, and I felt that you were feeling the same way.

I wandered lonely as a cow, Wordsworth wrote, then changed it to cloud: this early summer, the second without you home, is the saddest of our lives.

I've been lucky, you said, the other day — one of the glass shanks cutting at the L-shaped scar.

Then, How is your husband? and, to my mother, Heather, I want to come home.

Dad, last night I dreamed that I was you. Everyone talked differently to me, and it was frightening; the blurry world heaved and stammered.

I was lying there crying, and in the morning your eyes were red, and Mom asked why.

AND ALL OF YOUR ART

The things you made are tied up with your accidents.

When you fell asleep driving and smashed into a truck, you were in the hospital so long, and I was too little to visit.

Mom had me stand on the lawn and you stood at the window and waved.

Then you taught yourself origami, and sent me flowers.

You learned to make stained-glass lamps and pictures: your hands were always cut up and healing.

You made collages, and kept a sketch pad filled with oil pastel studies of skulls, drapery, and stone archers.

You built shelves and walls and rooms, collected stones for a year to build a perimeter around your house, constructed with much falling and crashing.

I don't know what happened before the self-portrait you sent me, where you are looking impassively forward, your forehead bisected by a livid red scar.

Your father scares me with all of his scars!

And he looks like a boxer, the classmate I went to Girl Guides with said just before I quit.

He wore his hair a little long then, with sideburns; a black leather car coat with a wine-coloured silk lining.

He stopped making things, discounting his strange garden, some time ago.

The last time we sat there together, he had me choose one of the three tiny pines as my own.

I check for it when I am there, and am relieved to see it is full and green; that it has not grown an inch.

Nothing has changed, Dad.

Your mind draws a forest then drags a black crayon through it: this is the way out.

THE HAYLOFT

My sister came to see my father for his birthday, exactly one week before mine.

I have sent him CDs to replace the ones that have been stolen again, along with his pillow, blankets, shirts and pants.

There is a little party on the Thursday: they sing all of "American Pie," his favourite song, after he unwraps the jewel case.

I have the phone on speaker, and am barely awake.
This will be the day that I die, I sing along, while rubbing toothpaste on my gums.

Later, my father was in the Hayloft, about to be executed.

I have to hang up and stop that, I said, and he said, That's my girl.

Tonight he says the blank spaces are getting bigger, and that he won't be here much longer.

You know that I will always take care of you, my father would say, when things were bad.

The blank spaces have blotted out almost everything; after fourteen years alone, when someone touches me, I flinch.

When will you come see me? he asks.

I miss you, he says, and I say it back, but this time we are both miserable because what we are saying is that who we were and what we were is gone.

MY FATHER'S FIRST GIRLFRIEND

She loved Gibson's illustrations, and lent my father a big hardcover of his work that
I took with me when I left home,

Always returning to the image of a man at a dinner party
making bread pills between an amorous couple.

Someone stole the book, I am ashamed to say how many things are gone,
places, people.

Barbara dated my dad when they were teenagers, and that is almost all I know
except, my mom tells me, they must have met at the stables;

That my dad loves riding horses: I never knew.

I imagine her as a dark-eyed brunette in a stiff black dress, her hair falling over her
face like a veil —

The other day, my father said that her husband killed himself.

I hope she doesn't get an idea like that, he said, worried.

But it was her, it was Barbara who killed herself.

I don't know why or how.

There are two pages, in the sketch pad, covered with charcoal sketches of speedy
horse races.

Art is what made them lean in, at some point, two dark beauties.

He has never mentioned her before. She has always wrung her ghastly hands
like the stylish man tearing bread apart between the couple fastened together,

Then transforming the white fluff into them, into angels into angels.

— mors certa, hora incerta

YOUR VOICE, ON THE RECORDING

Well, you hurt your head, I say, in the recording labelled TUE APR 14 7:55 P.M.
And you have a hard time walking.

I do?

And you can't really see.

Jesus Christ, I'm a wreck!

No, no.

I feel sad.

Why?

I feel left out of things. All the time.

The recording ends.

I listened to it late last night, and deleted it. By accident, I guess.
But the memory of his admission is bad enough.

Other memories —

You close your eyes and face the wall when we leave, though you aren't sleepy.

Or, when I came to see you and you were asleep: your eyes webbed shut and
nesting in dark, lined skin like a turtle's

Popped open and before you could compose yourself your whole face burst into the
biggest smile.

Dad, you were just lying there in that warm, empty room, dressed in the lime-
green and lemon-yellow shirt and your dreams were good ones, and I, then
        everyone, was there.

AUGUST'S END

In two days, our summer will pass, summer of Leos, of we two loafers
whose crossed feet show the genome's instructions:

The toes of the high-arched feet will contract and extend.

Your voice is more frantic these days: I am trapped in a maze, you said.

I told you about the time I went to a huge maze in Niagara Falls and got lost.
Angrily, I kicked the side down and stepped onto the road.

I walk around, buying little things after another day of complete silence, just
little things

Like a cake of soap that says Debbie that showcases a pretty brunette; a jar of
rosewater, a book about Allen Ginsberg, four dinosaurs.

Stepped among sizzling crud and pigeons pecking around an ancient dog,
stumbling beside his crippled owner, a soiled mask and an open

Refrigerated panel truck, filled with stiff, rose-pink pigs.

The Parkdale rat invasion is all over the news, forcing the memory of a man — who
had drawn a crowd of mothers and babies and other passersby — beating a rat to
    death in a trash can.

Oh, why? You are terrible people, I said, and one mother slowly backed away.

Or stories of other rats guided through mazes, their times charted until, having
worked it all out, they are killed.

Why — the agitation in my father's voice is the sound of something trapped.

There is a maze and he can get through it, but it still doesn't matter.

Kick the wall down, I say, but he has dropped the phone.

IN THE PICTURE

You are wearing a black suit and crisp white shirt, your black hair is slicked back past the widow's peak,

You are reaching into your breast pocket for something and I am sitting beside you in a ruffled white dress with short red hair and little bangs:

Our identical eyes cut the camera like blue shanks.

I am waiting for the cement ceiling to fall on me and finish me off, you said tonight.

It is loose and swaying, layers and layers.

Go tell the engineer! I say to my mother: this is a new thing we do; listening to him, that is.

My mother leaves on her mock errand, and Dad tells me he is just waiting (is he really waiting?) for the other shoe to drop.

I know what you mean, I say, involuntarily.

I have been taking long, crazed walks every day, to avoid thinking. It is a heat wave: by the end, I am filthy and defiant: no showers!

Yesterday, I went back to the Dollarama, and saw a shelf of single plastic ladies' pumps, dispensing tape.

At night, I flinch, thinking of a black heel breaking my nose, of drowning in blood, and still,

This has nothing on what you have been through.

Maybe sleep with a pillow on your head? I say, knowing the pillow and fleecy case I got him were stolen long ago,

And he says, OK. He is exhausted, but trying very hard to be nice.

In the photograph he is smiling enough to bare the gap in his teeth that I will also inherit, and letting a bit of light into his eyes.

He is a handsome new father, after all.

His life feels like a ride through space that has barely started.

He is reaching for a gun.

He uses it to shoot himself, having seen the way he will be punished.

He moves me to the floor first.

I am trapped in the warm, clinging rain.

No, it was just a cigarette to have with a glass of whisky; that whisky would have its way with him, over time.

In the good dreams, in the fourth glass, the Comets play and the room fills with dancing kids: one dips and her crinolines are the Aurora Borealis.

He is reaching for his boutonniere, the chilly flower he will pin to his collar before taking my alluring, blond mother's hand, and leading her to the floor,

Slowly: they are just getting started.

SUNDOWN

The sun is still blazing when we speak, but by 5 p.m. you start sundowning.
I read about it, how fatigue and hunger play a part, other things.

You are desperate to hang up, and though you try to be civil, you unfailingly
find a way to end our talk,

And if I say, like I did today, But don't you want to talk to me, you cry out, I'm
confused. Please — call me later.

And so I hurt him, angry and greedy for the voice I have followed all my life.

Leave me alone! I snap at my weeping dog: how quickly my solicitous fear
is purified into rage.

Anger is an energy I inform the gutters beneath my eyes, myself, as I patrol the
house and street with a baseball bat, sort of elated.

In the early evening, the shadows start to form and dreams are burned into the
truth.

Your eyes go black as well, all there is are sounds, dark pulsing squares and the
smell of pork and urine,

Making cunning prisons where you are whipped until you bend.

I am sitting by my window, watching an old video of Gordon Lightfoot
in patched jeans and an embroidered shirt, singing about this.

He says, dejected, of sundown that he feels like he's winning when he's losing again.

I try to zap this gentle performance to you, thinking of the time I gave you a record
that I liked for Christmas,

And came across you, months later, resting your back against the stereo console,
holding a drink and listening to one of the sadder songs, your eyes closed.

I pray that your eyes are closed as the terrors take on form and sound; that your lonely heart finds a song that sticks to you like honey,

That you are lowered into safety, as you lap it from your great, still paws.

Always injured, never killed, my father says by way of hello.

He then says he will let me go, then: I hear him tell my mother, She sounds so bored. She didn't even say how are you?

I'm sorry, I say. I tried. The phone dies in my hand.

The summer is slouching to its finish, dragging its dirty nets.

I saw the first of the new rat bodies yesterday, emptied and flattened so thoroughly, it looked like a grey felt cut-out, its eyes scissored into shock-wide holes.

Intermittently, a terrible band on the waterfront will burst into some voodoo, scudded here by the wind and I confabulate —

I woke up on the fifth day in the shoebox, where a well-meaning child has placed me on a bed of grass, sick with fever.

The girl brings me cheese slices and water, cringes at my broken, bleeding leg.

I sleep more and more and in my dreams God says, *You're done for* and *It only gets worse.*

One whole day she forgets me, and I can see I am starting to sicken her.

There is movement: I bump-bump around the box, soaked and miserable, then the lid is torn away and the vastness of the black sky, its firmament of golden light

Envelops me as I am tilted to the grass, as she calls back, I'm sorry, I tried.

This grass is alive and clean: I roll onto my spine and wave my feet, gently. I expose my injury to the glowing eyes all around,

The *tapetum lucidum* in the green and yellow,
reflecting me also: my rat thoughts.

Injured, but never killed! I think as I scuttle into a hole, and vanish.

Samson is my father's cat, adopted at a fair. The sign on his cage said that he had "BIT A CHILD."

My father reached into his cage and the cat rolled over, smiling: This cat would never hurt anyone, he said.

I will never know what happened the last night my father was still himself.

He was always awake in the middle of the night, crashing around, maddened by good smells and the small lights of his basement den — a room I can't remember

Without thinking of my brother's furious discovery of moths in the carpet at midnight, and the subsequent hours spent moving the squares he hacked it into,

Some soft-covered books, boxes of toys, no, my mother already got rid of those, and so many other of his things —

Once, he ripped his arm from its socket, falling down the stairs and grabbing the banister; he must have fallen again.

I think of Samson lying like a sneak on the stairs, and shake my head, because he loves him.

He and I are great fallers: how is it that he didn't get up this time?

Get up, as we do, and inspect the damage, then walk slowly back to whatever caught our attention,

A burned-out bulb, an album on a shelf, a jar of peanut butter.

Tonight, I am too ashamed to tell him how things have turned. That I have not been out of bed in days: I have the flu, I say.

We're both in the hospital, he says, sweetly, I remember that.

I remember that, he says, that I am sick, and he is worried
it will take a lot less to knock me over.

I am already down, carelessly looking through notes, like the bear hat
he wore to Dorval station to wave me off, while giving me the excellent advice to

Try not to fight, but I was already into it with the porter as I held up my hand
from the car, at the big tough man with purled ears,

A knitted snout soft on his shattered forehead.

This is the address of our first house, a corner lot, initially, in a housing development that went broke.

Maisons des Érables was carved out of the forest crawling off the Trans-Canada —
an elevated grid of creamy A-frames, made sinister by long squiggles of dirt road, massive

Squares of dark woods and the beating current of the murky Richelieu river, sludging past the foot of the hills.

I shared a room with my baby sister, who stamped around with a bone in her hair, breaking my things and throwing around the little king and queen of her Fisher-
Price court.

I would underline passages in *Helter Skelter*, then get the tool box and fix the sliding doors, watch wolves lope by with babies in their mouths,

Shirtless maniacs writing *PIG* with stones in our backyard, devils out of Hell.
I was afraid all the time and furious, until my father decided to tackle the basement.

He put up drywall, and laid down a floor, then broadloom, added a wall of cork, a built-in bookshelf, a recessed bureau and an adjacent bathroom.

Best of all, he added two locks, for home and away.

This is still my favourite room, Dad. With dozens of pin-ups on the cork, and my old Brother stereo; a shelf of makeup, a *Serpico* poster over the bed and vanilla incense burning.

We barely spoke in my mid-teens: how did you know?

School was hard: I wasn't cute. More significantly, I have always wanted to be on my own, but loved anyway.

The love is evanescing as I write you, flattening out like the acres of trees chopped down, until I call, and you are well, and speak so kindly.

And I understand what I always forget, that you carved out this space for me because you know me, and

You still love me.

When I started graduate school, and started publishing, you were always interested in my stories about cruel colleagues, vile professors,

The terror that was my comprehensive exam, covering "Beowulf to Virginia Woolf" with no reading list or counsel other than "Astonish us."

When I failed one of them, I came home and found a hidden stairwell in my apartment building; I sat there for hours, ashamed and nauseated.

You made study binders for me and the group I met with only twice; when my cat peed on all of my notes, you spent a whole day at your office photocopying each page,

And returned them as a clean copy, with another envelope labelled "Cat Treated Originals."

My readings, the magazines I showed up in: you asked me everything about them, and laughed about the writers I called the Blouse, Jolene and Crab Legs.

You stopped asking me anything at all a year or so before you got sick.

I told you something twice, and you asked why I was so needy.

Maybe the illness was already there.

Or is it that you were tired of my monstrous desire for your approval?

This week, I lost the last of my little jobs; my book was shunned with Mennonite conviction,

A book I wrote as though it were burning and only my constant vigilance would keep it alight.

So my sick dog and I slept for another day until I was able to go out and, like a fly, secure something sweet and sticky,

And I talked to you and you were as nice as always: I want to see you!

The whole time my mind is cut into a razor and the razor is dying to do damage: every time I visit you, I rest beside you and want to stay.

PUMPKIN

You brought home the biggest pumpkin ever in St-Hilaire, and rolled it onto the porch.

It was four feet high and around, easily; you would cut it the night before Halloween,
with your expert triangle-eyes and row of spooky teeth.

It was all we could talk about.

Two days before October the thirty-first, someone stole it.

You just got another, smaller one, making do like the year when we lived in the Ville
d'Anjou apartment, and you cut up one that was rotten on the bottom and placed
    it in a wicker basket.

And we all felt sad in silent ways. Even now, I feel badly when I see
you spotting the big orange ball at a fair, and pulling over,
    wanting to amaze us.

Of you then driving home with the pumpkin beside you, keeping crazy company,
as you made the long trip back.

The year the FLQ were at large, you took me out on Halloween — I was a cat, I was
always a cat —

And painted Jimmy a soldier's uniform out of a big paper bag from a pattern in one
of Mom's magazines.

Every year you handed out candy, and sneaked some of ours:

I see the big pumpkin strapped to the seat, its stem curving towards the window,
and it shines, there is a moon in your car,

A hunter's moon, its flesh alight for the stealthy killers crossing worlds of
pine needles and scorched riverbeds,

Making the long trip towards you, with a dreadful map and crossbows
in their hands.

WHAT IS REMEMBERED

I'm quite uncomfortable, but I'll see you in England later on today, my father said this morning.

I will call to him again at dinnertime, and he will be too distraught to talk, or too caught up, catching bandits or escaping from the black room they have filled with explosives.

He may not want to speak to anyone but the police; he may say hello, his voice increasingly anxious to be done with the stultifying conversation.

His memory is cut away more every day, some of which I understand.

It is like looking at old pictures of him and me, on rafts or at tables loaded with sugar cookies: I don't have a clue where we were or how I felt,

Except safe, except loved: I can't help him this way, he is too angry, too distraught.

We had bad times, but they are receding now too, in my own imperfect mind: they sit in their shell, beneath a whorl of mouse-coloured hair —

Once, I split my head wide open, and a month later my dad found a stitch they had forgotten and eased it out with tweezers,

I remember this!

He is also brilliant at taking out splinters: nothing ever slides under my skin, no spoke of wood, no needle of glass, without me crying for my father.

When my father cries, when he is alone, it is because he remembers.

And doesn't: You smell like a hooker, he told my mother, who was wearing L'Air du Temps, the perfume he gave her.

I always liked that smell, he said.

THE BUTTERFLY

I did this for you, for all the birds and strays you coaxed home, for the time you
killed a spider and were miserable, its blood on the wall over your bed

You called "stigmata" and would not clean off.

The monarch was lying in a parking lot on one of these awful September days,
where the sun feels bald and incensed and everything is putrid.

I coaxed it onto a paper, and dropped it. Two black spots on its wings: he crawled
on my foot and I reached for him.

He latched on to my finger and I carried him to a shrub and left. Came back,
with my heavy bags of FreshCo food, and lifted him again.

We walked all the way home and I made him a habitat in a big iron cage, filled with
grass and honey-water, fruit-water, a slice of peach.

That day and night we became good friends: I fed him with a baby spoon.
He was often hiding; I became very nervous.

I went out for a while and I brought home red milkweed.

He was lying on the floor, over a smear of green.

I gave him the flower and he burst it, the thick white juice flowed and he clutched
my finger; I returned him to the cage and he fell on his side.

He was dead.

I watched him for twenty-four hours.
Buried him, then dug up the box, terrified he was still alive.

I asked God for a miracle and two monarchs appeared, bouncing in the sky.

I called him Buddy.

Your father had a bird named Buddy, my mother said. Some old pigeon who visited him every morning.

I am making bigger mistakes, each day.

You are going to die alone, my father said, in a terrible argument we had, some summers ago.

We all die alone, I said to him — still, my little friend waited so long for me to return, and feed and return him

To his final place in the sun by a tall, skinny tree and a dragon kite that shoots colour like explosives everywhere —

I said to him, feeling his hand attach itself to mine.

I call my family and tell them what prizes I didn't get: no big blue ribbon for this hog.

The tradition isn't the same anymore: today, I looked up more jokes, and read them to my barely awake father.

"Do you see that castle?" the third bat said. "Well I didn't," is the end of one that causes Dad to say, Go away and leave me alone.

We all have colds, fever dreams: Christ comes to us in a sports coat and sandals and says, I'm sorry, but there is nothing joyful ahead.

I haven't changed in days: I languish in my filthy, tangled weave and torn rayon slip.

Puffy pill sacraments, Wonder bread and large-print Sidney Sheldon novels: Oh my darling, let's make the universe roar!

A guy on the streetcar told me, Stop fucken talking to yourself so much, and I was frightened, as I was sure I wasn't.

I even mouthed, He's CRAZY, at the other obvious criminal beside him.

I embrace this now: needled into the arrow of time I propose is a *curve*, I and my movie-star boyfriend visit Paris where I speak French and slap his ass with
    baguettes;

Where he brings home, over his arms like dying women, gold-beaten gowns with gemstones set in the straps; red-and-black lingerie covered in Chantilly lace:

When I am an old man and I meet you at the Fan Expo in Toronto, I will act oblivious, he says.

We must not agonize the world with our timeless ardour.

Oui, c'est vrai, mon amour, je comprends absolument, I say as I call Mom's cell and she is cross because of her cold and my father bleats and Francis snores, always sleepy
  these days.

The heater zzzes along until it is time for a peanut butter sandwich and the conviction that tomorrow is the really good day, at last.

The day my father gets up and drives here without stopping and Frank is so young he jumps on springs to see him through the window,

And I still have friends: money flies through the air like confetti, my books come with gold stickers that say WINNA WINNA,

My combed, clean hair falls to my shoulders.

I call my millionaire boyfriend and tell him that I scarcely noticed him in *Easy A* and Malcolm? I say, like the happy opposite of the telegram in Jackie Susann's

The Love Machine, terminated as the author's cancer grew black branches inside her,

I don't need you.

IT'S ALL OVER NOW

The metal zils and high black keys usher in a sick dream of the past
moving slowly, like an ectoderm folding over,

Interminable days, my long face in the black window split in two.

I ask if you would like to see me on Halloween. We could dress up, I say, but you
don't want to, and I remember you have always hated to look foolish.

Let's get that stripper in here again, you say, and I laugh.

That night, Mom left the drawers unlocked and you ate five Cherry Blossoms.

I ate too many, you tell me the next day. Ooof. My stomach hurts.

I am telling everyone I am in the emergency room, and by everyone I mean
the one or two people who still call.

If they wonder why my dog is snoring beside me there, they don't say.

I will bandage my wrists where I want the cuts to go, nice vertical sticks, and
remember the blood flowing just as sweetly, Dad.

These are not things that I tell you.

You ask how I am, or how my band is, and I say, Fine, thinking of my imaginary
cover band, where I play lead guitar and extract a song

That says that it's all over now,

The blue things —

It pours instead, in the picture of us, underneath umbrellas in your backyard,

Mom captured us, as we played up our distress, as we stood on the stairs on the
verge of

Stepping inside and shaking like dogs and my own dog running in circles and bread rising and *only* good things now,

Your egg-fragile head nestled into a soft, downy pillow and the song starting up again in an aurora of chimes.

WHAT I AM AFRAID OF

I don't want to sleep, the night is the kind of soggy dross that comforts me.
Or wake up, since Francis sleeps most of the day now,

And Blaze and I are at his head and feet; I can feel his pulse in one paw with my
finger, which beats us back into the dreams of everything we have left behind

On shore, friends and more than friends, meetings and work and seeing people,
the life I struggled to have for so long.

I try to stay clean and speak to my father two times a day, to set out the kids'
dinner, and make something small for myself,

Stack the bills and letters from collection agencies by the unwashed clothes and
reminders of things left undone, unfixed, unfinished,

Hide from the sun's rebuke, make a list of everyone not speaking to me, calls not
returned, stop:

I am just sick and weak, or pathetic and lazy.

Either way, there has not been a single good day — those rare, yet reliable
patches — since you fell down the stairs, crashing and crying out,

Since no one heard you or saw the blood filling your skull and you asked,

What time is it? until an ambulance arrived, taking you to certain negligence.

I was seeing old friends that night, and I walked home slowly, thinking that love
has a memory, an amiable thought dispelled by SIX MISSED CALLS,

And you having barely any memory at all, none, I pray, of the pitiless wooden floor
bashing your face, and not yielding.

Your legs moving slowly like feelers, afraid, I am afraid of monsters,
of losing track, of time.

WE HAVE STOPPED

Reading about dementia entirely, or blindness; stopped making agitated calls to various agencies; stopped making you intriguing and helpful things.

My mother is my conduit to Dad, and only friend. Oh it's so sad, so sad, she says, when I tell her about my own dangerous enemies,

The stocks and manacles; the horrified, contented whispers.

I suppose she thinks she deserves better!

I have just gone outside for the first time in three days. I met a pit bull named Dante and his friend, a big guy with a shock of black hair, who laughed,

We laughed when Dante barked as I took his picture.

I bought Frank's dinner: it was a long night of him walking painfully from one pillow to the next, so ill that Blaze walked up to him and as I held my breath

My feral cat held and kissed him.

I finished Duolingo, and called the *Centre d'Hébergement*: Please speak French, I asked the nurse, who did, then grew impatient: Your father is agitated and does like he always does.

But when we talked earlier he was so kind, I felt my brittleness fall apart.

Why is your mother so sad? he said, and I told him that she missed him, that we all did, and he said, You had better not be kidding me.

Lui dire que je l'aime, I practice saying, and *Pourriez-vous s'il vous plaît essayer de l'aimer?*

Touch his head, where the new, auburn hair has grown, and its softness will change you, *je les exhorte.*

Good night, *Contre les cauchemars, mon cher.*

If I live like you, disconnected and sleeping, always sleeping; occasionally widening my eyes and shouting HELP HELP HELP HELP HELP

At the one who seems asleep Himself, in the warm grass among the fleecy lambs.

If I lose all my jobs, which get in the way of the pain and the painkillers and the sleep, and waken only for bread and paste,

And the occasional, dreadful indignity.

They are painting me, my father said. Like a car is what he meant.
They're on the second coat.

What colour? I asked, and he said, Grey.

Then he took his sandwich filled with dynamite and pushed it away.

The bombs in the walls are set to go off in three minutes, he told me as I looked, bleakly, at an array of pawnshop jewels,

Past the cathedral covered in blue scaffolding and the pop-up Halloween store, filled with outfits for streetwalkers.

I was going somewhere, after a week inside.

I come home to my dog, who is sleeping as always, unless he is trying to get up or down, or switch positions.

I call later and the nurse says, *Oui, il a mangé, et oui, il a mangé de la crème glacée que votre mère a laissée pour lui.*

If I think long enough about his mouth filled with this cold blessing, I can sleep again: in that world, there is room enough and time.

AND FLY AWAY

More and more, my father sounds like a kid being forced to talk to an odious relative, he is that anxious to hang up,

I can see him jumping up and down on noodle legs and squishing the phone like a bug.

If he is defeated, like today, he will want to tell me, and not want to tell me, how the boys made him eat shit sandwiches,

"Right out of the toilet."

These times, he is so sad, I can find the truth of what he is saying glint in the filth of the sifting pan.

He used to count on me to help him and has given up, too shrewd to believe I have friends on the bomb squad, that I know killers for hire.

I am just a necessary irritant, like peanut butter on stale bread, thinly spread, that he wants but cannot stand

The indignity: our interactions are useless, but fraught with love.

Who did this to you? I ask him as we fly off and the building and the Oratory's spike become blurred.

Everyone, he says, but his pain is passing.

A vector of birds has included us and they are beautiful.

When some are taken by shots fired, he cries out, but the south is in sight: what good times we will have, landing there and skimming

The sun-blessed waves for fish.

傷
感

I wrote you a letter inside a card: Chinatown at dusk all honeyed vermicelli and sweet pears,

And never mailed it; when the moon-smudged faces appear, now and then, on one of the masses of paper in what was once my office, I am glad.

It was about me, as always, and you not caring: *I feel like you don't love me anymore.*

Stuck piglet, skinned and hanging behind glass, the man in the crimson apron.

I never asked why you had retreated; I didn't help you when you couldn't move anymore from the pain,

When you phoned and phoned, I tried to think clearly, then sent you some pills.

The night the call came, I was passing the railroad tracks and smiling.
You look beautiful, my friend William had said;

I could have leaned against the piss wall of the underpass, screaming sparks.

I was at your hospital in a day, how you looked — your eyes fugitive, your loose skin pulled up and stapled back,

How desperately you needed us: it has been two years now. We have not saved you.

We do not talk or pray or hope; there are no cheerful pictures in your room, there is nothing but a wandering old lady who loves you ("Such a nice kid")

And music, when you can stand it.

The night I arrived at your house, I put on your jacket, a windbreaker silkscreened with Ali's face, and put my hand in the pockets.

I had been writing an article for a month, about Erin Gilmour, a young woman
who was murdered thirty years ago, and I had talked a bit about it to you,

About speaking with her brothers, and her dad.

Her father told me she came to him in a vision and insisted that he get on with his
life, and he did.

The day it was published, I called home, and we talked a bit.

In your pocket is a receipt from the Costco on Transcanada Nord.

At 11:21 a.m., Vicki R. rang in a *Poulet Rôti*, 48 Duracell AA batteries and a copy of
Maclean's.

You never told me that you bought it: I hold the sacred receipt then return
it to the side of the bureau that faces the bed I rarely leave, where I have

Pinned up pictures of you and me and Frankie, your ward's number
and extensions, a few cards Mom has had you sign, in tilted, still-elegant script.

That father was so secure in his conviction; still, I felt the little coffin that lives
inside him, Dad,

The rush of your trip, so proud of me, the careful way you would have read what I
wrote and grieved the girl and her father.

How I grieve you, living, never to read again, or speak to me, even on the *good
days*, without asking me things I cannot answer, or won't.

You cared about me too much: I am reduced to calling you from outside, jagging
through traffic and saying, Darling, I know, when I don't, until you,

Gracefully, let me off the hook.

Thank you, you tell me, with a wobble in your voice, and I hurry you off the phone: there is that fat man again, drinking Lakeport, who I want to photograph.

I want to take pictures of him in his LCBO bag-crown, bang my heart with my fist, and get that fucker going.

MY FATHER'S MOTHER

Was inclined to spoil my dad a bit: she ordered him shirts and ties and books, and her death equalled negative space below the tree, or on the table.

She was a rare admirer of mine, as well: so often, my father's mother, Helen, swells past me in silvery streaks,

Catching my desolate questions like a spiral of glue, why I am so disliked and why there is cruelty, and why him?

She sees his scarred head and his eyes, absent of their ferocity and warmth, and draws sky-blue wool from a velvet bag embroidered with tiny flowers

And knits him two soft stones, the colour of the asters, the clematis and blue stars that climb the hill of her garden.

I'll come and help you, my father still says to me. I'll drive over, send me the forms.

My dog has a lump on his neck the size of a doorknob.

We rarely wake up, except to talk to Dad, who prays for him, then worries again about the *Shenoi Boy*, the poisoners, and lighters of fires.

What would my grandmother say to me, besides Get out of bed?

Nothing at all, but there are her arms, draped in the velour I call velvet, reaching, and there are her kind eyes, welded shut from watching her son dying.

Sometime after the blow, a small stream collects in the pan: my life is that
slick, unctuous trickle and someone,

Is it God, yelling, Don't pour that in the sink!

Should we call the kids? my mother says, and my father says, What's the point, if
I'm never leaving this place?

I open the hinged golden heart that is his head.

Plucked from a French church, it encloses fervid prayers, *Cher Dieu, je Te prie de Te
rappeler certains cas*—

My father used to paint my mother's nails, one pearly foot in his big, broken hand,
the brush sweeping up roses, catkins, anemones.

That's enough and today, after days of being burned and tied to a net while the
other players took slapshots at his face and he said he wished he knew what it was
    to be dead,

He said, Hello baby, to me, and I heard him smile.

(I prayed for this heart to swallow, Amen.)

Somewhere, in one of the many boxes and bags; the circle suitcases and truncated shelves; the towers of ephemera, chests, drawers,

Is the glossy binder my father gave me about the artist who made *Papa*, a sculpture that stands by my front door.

It is made out of driftwood, the whorls and fissures intact, and depicts a man pointing sternly with one arm;

The other holds a heraldic torch that keeps falling off in thuds that frighten the cat, and nettle me.

The father's head looks like a newel post: it is featureless and smooth, with pencilled-on eye circles and a line for a mouth: are these my dad's designs?

I think of the "eye rings" of grisly Old English poetry, of the triangles my father sliced into pumpkins, Euclid bowing discreetly beside him,

Notice, after two years, an organically formed baby pressed to the father's chest, made of darker, textured wood, puffing like a mushroom,

A camellia on a stout woman's heavy cheviot coat.

The day after my birthday, a neighbour asked me over. He had not come to my party, and I thought he meant to make a little celebration.

What happened? he said, eyes glittering: I heard you and your dad yelling and thought — The rest is merely noise, the millipede feet of my distaste, scuttling forward.

I didn't answer, just drained my bourbon and drain cleaner, and left.

What happened is that I hated my present, the statue, and made fun of it.

Mortified, my father lashed out at me, and though he came to my party, he didn't speak to me all night.

He stood beside me once, at the table where I sat, unmoving, as if holding on to the great love that he or I could seldom remember or respect.

That I couldn't, I mean.

He took a taxi back with a friend and talked about the same ex he still remembers with an affection I don't understand.

Ah well, give the great man my love, Tony says, sometime later, and I do.

Inside the album: small galleries from "Maine to Florida to Canada" are entranced by Lithuanian artist Parnis Baltuonis's "intriguing tree root sculptures of many sizes and shapes."

The roots are prised by the muscular artist "out of lakes and rivers and from the earth."

When Baltuonis sells a piece, he is dismayed. "In a sense it breaks his heart," his wife says, as she stands before a piece called *Wild Girl*.

My father is in quarantine today: someone has a gastrointestinal virus. The day before, he dropped the phone and I heard him plead with my mother not to leave him.

As soon as she leaves, they come in with belts: Listen to my heart, he said. It's beating like a hammer.

I'm scared, he said, as if surprised by the word.

They used to bind him with thick canvas ties, in the early days: he is remembering this, and the mean boys, and his helplessness.

Still he stands, having folded me into his chest, threatening everyone who comes near the door, my father of the lake and his wild girl.

What have you done to your life? he said, on my birthday, not unreasonably. He had dressed up in Bermuda shorts, a Mick's Gym tee and white sunglasses,

The last day I saw him, sad but not sick, his arms filled with the statue, his replacement, and I heard the voice I always turn over in my head like a coin,

I will always take care of you. You never have to worry.
In a sense this breaks my heart, that cold bounder!

THE NICE YOUNG MAN IN YELLOW AND GREEN

At FreshCo, where I have started crying and am chagrined, letting my cheap
mascara bleed and bawling like an old beast being lashed

(*I'm sorry I'm sorry,* the mule gasps, wanting the sting of the whip, wanting to feel
the physicality of disgust and hate)

There is a nice young man, who wears his lime-green and yellow colours well,
who makes a big show of moving away from me, then stoops to gather

Everything I knock over in my fat reaching.

He apologizes, looking demurely away from the black mush, from my eyes:
everyone is buying such nice things, I don't understand

What it is to love yourself this way, with tiny sugared doughnuts and glazed buns,
jars of persimmon jam, tins of coloured sprinkles.

It has been four days since they quarantined my father.

I have to tell him I won't see him at Christmas, that I'm not sure when I can visit.

I won't tell him that "I'm ruined" or what other terrors bellow inside me.

Dad, what I would tell you is this, if I could:

I took Francis to see Santa at a pet store that gives the photo money to the Humane
Society, an event I always forget.

I dressed him in a red sweatshirt, and we went out for the first time in months.
It turns out that he can't walk anymore,

So I carried him to the streetcar and onto the lap of the thin, unsmiling Santa,
and the girl with the clipboard said to the photographer,

who was calling his name,

He's fifteen, he can't hear, and laughed.

Then I carried him home and we ate honey drops and snacks, and he looked a bit confused but lovely.

I don't dream anymore, my grandmother, Mary, once said, and yes, I think, yes, I understand.

I am standing by the bags of candy, dreamless but for this: Don't take them away, and Don't let them hurt anymore,

And, Forget about me.

Once, in high spirits, I flirted with the young man, and he seems to have remembered; Christ, in the colours of a caterpillar,

What misery you take in, like the insides of broken flowers, their milk.

1975

I have kept up with my lessons, and they let me speak French for the first time
today *et je parlais à mon père à midi.*

*Il était inquiet au sujet de certains des criminels, mais quand je lui ai dit, Je t'appellerai
plus tard, a dit,*

Appele-moi tout le temps.

I will call, and be cautious not to say what is on my mind, like shaky dog legs: an
old associate writing, "Lynne, there is no work for you."

There is no "e" is all I say, it seems.

My knees, emptied of cartilage, look like bat caves and ache,

Bills I hide like painted eggs; unreturned letters and calls;

My book already remaindered: inside it lies all of my desire.

My father on a slippery bed with a plastic pillow, and nothing else.

My own bed, which I seldom leave, my bed of books and crumbs,
doggie toys and knitted blankets.

I buried myself into the rats' nest last night and watched Jack Nicholson,
who looks like my father, get taken down by the mental institution,

The same vee on his head, the stark confusion.

A movie I saw in 1977: this cauterized the last of my tears,
because it's too sad.

There's no use tracing the obvious, how wild, beautiful men and battered,
once-lovely women are made to be whipped.

My pop was real big, the Chief says; he did like he pleased. That's why everyone worked on him.

I think of my father, big as the world; dry-eyed, I think of the world's colours being scraped away with a curette, of its stitched-over rivers and cratered poles.

SKIN JOB

The space between us widens: I will not see you at Christmas.
My chair is magnetized, Lynn, come and help me, please.

I will miss watching your sightful hands, opening boxes of candy and scarves
and other crap, bells taped to the paper, things described to you;

You, trying to look like anything matters.

The scalding hot tray heavy with turkey medallions and wet stuffing;
Sofi in a Santa hat, various insensate people in Santa hats,

Like weeping willows with trash bags trapped in their branches.

Last week I dreamed I tried to take you swimming, in a hotel filled with tiny, fancy
people in spangled suits.

You fought in the hotel lobby instead, over a game of cards.

How hard we fight —

I have written this book for two years, too, written it against your leaving, or to
stay in the green raft where I sit, with you on the wharf, rocking me,

My face cat-calm and sun-yellow, my life in the distance.

I'm starting to shake off some of the cobwebs, you said yesterday, in a tremulous
voice.

Tonight, you will rage or you will cry because they are beating you again, or
burning your skin,

Forgetting you: Why does no one come to see me anymore? you asked my mother.
I don't feel real anymore, you said.

You were sick when you were my age, wondering what you had done with your life:
Nothing, nothing!

I did not know how to tell you then, that you are the most beautiful of the skin jobs, the one who is too human to prevail,

Who bleeds and rails from the rooftop, a white dove clenched in his hand, about what *you people* cannot imagine.

That all he has seen, he knows, as the sky opens,

Will disappear, *like tears in rain.*

And I will be the bird you let go, flying fast, my own time winding down also.

Two blue eyes shut; two blue fish dart underwater and are gone.

LATE DECEMBER

It seems so long since my brother and I visited you at the Jewish General,

Since you waved your hands and conjured a barn filled with people, assembled for the Pray-down.

You were more my father then, and less: each day your sweetness lands like a hand on my small back, holds me in the crèche of your arms.

Mom does not talk about private things, but chokes on tears. *I miss my Dougie*, she says, and clams up.

You had wanted to go to art school, which was preposterous to all concerned. Still, you drew and worked in different mediums;

Brought home cork balls from your father's machinist shop,

One of which you carved into a face — is it your face? — and coloured in with fine, near-psychedelic lines.

Made a collage of paper triangles, stained-glass windows and lamps, the origami flowers.

Smaller things, three pears in a blue bowl on the kitchen windowsill, glowing.

Every time I reach the top of the stairs, I grab your painted head and kiss it.

It is the memory of the pears' inner light and a child's first bouquet, no —

It is all the little things, like bees, that terrorize, so improbably; how lopsided angels become airborne.

JARDIN D'ENFANTS

Quand il y a quatre ans
mon père a lu un livre grand

Sans tous ses vêtements

Ses jambes en croix, un petit sourire
sur ses lèvres

Ma grand-mère, une femme propre,
a pris une photo

De ce singe fou.

La largesse du monde!

Et toutes ses lumières et dans ses yeux
qui flottaient ainsi

Dans la rivière mince, notre vie.

DECEMBER 24

My little dog looks hopeful: less or no crying today?

Some nights, I fill his mouth with water so he will swallow his pills and the water pours back red.

Hand, I say, when I reach to touch his face.

Kiss, Belly. Presents for you!

Somewhere along the way, I have filled a box with Christmas: vintage Peanuts ornaments; a bear in a tutu, or the angel; plump deer candles; four bulbs out of forty, not yet smashed.

All week, I have run around making a tiny holiday, scared of the violence of my depression, scared of God, who knows I am not sure why this day matters.

I see myself trim, in a fitted uniform, singing "Happy Birthday to Jesus" to two gauntlets of half-naked Marines, as I walk up the stairs of the church,

Trying doors, finding them locked, as usual, I bang my head against them until it rings and that is my prayer.

My family was unerring in their holiday traditions: tinsel had to be placed strand by strand on the tree,

The gifts hidden and excessive, the mess after dinner took hours to clean, making the meal nauseous with dread.

And every Christmas Eve, my dad read *The Night Before Christmas*, from the same old paperback,

Changing many of the lines to jokes more familiar than the stupid poem, reading in a big, billowy voice.

I came to feel uneasy then uncomfortable, listening.

I was so old, with no family of my own: it felt strange, walking through the same rituals.

The year I remember best was when I came home drunk to their Sherbrooke Street apartment, and Dad had been drinking heavily too:

He had misplaced the book, so he improvised a fantastically filthy, curse-loaded version that I basked in, more so when I saw the horrified, pinched faces of my sister and mother.

As the years stacked up, as I listened to you with a mixture of bad nerves and flat hope, I did not have the prescience to stand up and crown you,

Crown you with gold and jewels and say, Never stop reading to us, you are the funniest, kindest man in the kingdom.

I did not know to curl up like a fawn on the foot of the bed and let my father's words fall, like soft pine needles, and rise, like a shy satin moon,

To say, This is the meaning, to an attentive Jesus, listening also, to his dear child.

THE ROYAL BANK

Dad is on his own, in the dream cast early into my unholy sleep, so seven a.m., wearing summer clothes and attending a Royal Bank function,

He wrote a platform for them, my brother explained, as we drove to get him. He was walking slowly among the other guests, keeping close to the fence.

We moved towards him, on my mind what is always on my mind, to get him into the car and drive without stopping.

My mother called, and spoke loudly, her voice shrill. He *can* go to things on his own, can't he, Lynn? she said, wanting me to say yes.

That day she steered him, luffing, towards the bare bathroom and told me: I have been worried.

An ant with a breadcrumb ten times her size, brave enough to pilot for the others; a dotted pardalote pimping her nest with a slingshot.

She is the recipient of love letters and flowers and perfume,

Sent long ago by the diffident man in the sports shirt and slacks who, in the photograph she keeps in her drawer, is shrinking against the planks of a fence.

He can only see the occasional thing — *There are faces on my toes!* — my mother, in lovely pieces.

I woke up from an operation many years ago and her face was inches from mine and this was like coming to life among shouts of *Clear!*

And the sun, hemorrhaging over the sheets, and so beauty is delivered still.

SPEAK QUIETLY, THEY ARE LISTENING

You are nervous of being alone, you say. There are rats, rats that bite or listen in,
and so you whisper, I love you, and Goodbye,

In the little voice, and I hear in its rust that your voice strains tears all day and
night; your nose runs ceaselessly from sorrow.

You often won't eat, because they are trying to kill you; you are so tired, Dad, that
you can barely hold a conversation together, and I have so little to say.

When I am alone, I cry so loudly it is more like ragged screaming, and insensible:
Leave him alone! and *Why are you doing this?*

I curse my gentle God, who watches and places His irradiated fingers to His lips.

Let me go, to be with my Maker, you say on Thanksgiving, after a lunch
of blood-caked lamb.

Come with me, you say, and my mouth opens in assent.

There is not much time left, as far as I can tell, if the length of the (rigged, always
rigged) fights are any indication,

The watery lungs of my old dog; my own damnation.

But I ask every day for the Miracle. Or swat the shrine off the dresser,
and stamp on it.

Then let him find peace, I bargain, thinking of Dylan Thomas, and hating,
passionately hating, people's reverence for his arrogant poem;

Or good feelings, a memory: that is my final offer.

When you were born, my mother says, your father bought a pair of fuzzy dice for his car, and drove to get us at the hospital.

The dice were for luck. The tiny red rose he presented me at birth was for love. This memory, Dad. This is the one.

PEACE, LOVE, EMPATHY

We all brought in food on the last day of class, in grade one.

There were no names on the dishes, and someone left out a plate
of white sausages rolling in flecks of red cabbage.

We were repulsed and made a show of moving the cooties food
to the end of the table.

I laughed about it to my father that night, about what someone brought.

That's terrible, he said.
Imagine how that child felt, the one whose mother made the food.

Then I was ashamed and this is how I learned what empathy was, that it
is the mother up late after work, searing sausages and chopping cabbage,

A dish her family likes.

It is the mother's child, stuffing the food into a bag after everyone leaves, and
sliding it into the trash, furious at us, furious at her.

It is what is there and is not, indexically, verily: signifier and signified,

What I would understand later to mean the smell of fried cabbage and the green,
frilled head in one's hands.

The Alphabet Gang who are always at large: my father senses malice and death,
like a twelve-point buck passing a hunting blind.

After the operation, when we were all hopeful, he had to have some imaging done
that visibly frightened him: the weird room, the noise,

The cavalier attendant with his small, sallow moustache.

I spoke to him urgently. Please lie still and don't move, or they will keep making
you do it. It's not so bad, think of something nice.

Will you wait for me? he said, and I promised.
I watched from the corner of the room, saw his arms cross as he slid in,

His bare feet tremble then lie still.

He was in the metal tube for thirty minutes, with me and not.

I hurried him back to his room when it was done, racing his wheelchair
the way he likes — one time, I took him out the hospital door and started running.

My father taught me to love people I do not know; to feel —

That punch in the solar plexus you take when
the strongest person you know says, *Wait for me* and his words are loaded

With over seventy years of bravery, and what it costs.

Solitude, loneliness, the hard and heavy armature around

Your whole body, rigid with anxiety and will; glanced by the smallest blush,
something nice, someone waiting though neither of you can see.

— *Merci, Père, pour ton belle âme.*

WHEN SOMEONE DIES

At the *hébergement*, an "In Memoriam" announcement appears on the bulletin
board by the elevators, an area the patients are forbidden to enter,

A low-resolution photocopy, hovering above bits of news, like an upcoming
Matin de la musique et de la danse avec M. René Voltaire! or *Maïs ce
    week-end en torchis, deux par personne.*

The obituary information, in the one I have seen, was devoid of sentiment:
Monsieur Plouffe est décédé cette semaine, 1935–2016;

The accompanying photograph appears to have been taken at the morgue —
his eyes sewn shut; his mouth slack, skin loose and waffle-textured.

The nurses gobble in their station across the hall about *ce beau gars* or *quel beau
gars* as I carefully remove the announcement,

Bring it with me and, later, use a soft pencil to modify the features, add cheekbones
and a thatch of hair.

Monsieur Plouffe, I write, in heavy ink, *était brave et bon. Et il a enduré, et c'est tout. Il
était le père de quelqu'un, et je vous le dis, ma soeur, votre Coeur peut être réparé et
    rendu fort par votre souvenir de cet homme hors pair.*

I replace it the next day and it is taken down.

Someone else has died: another arctic elegy and ghoul has been pinned to the
board.

I find my notice, folded in the trash, and pluck it out.

I care about you, Mr. Plouffe, I tell the quilted paper, before releasing it like a
Viking ship into the kitchenette sink.

I cannot let you die here, I think, as I brush my father's still more russet-coloured
hair.

And if you did, I would hold the staff hostage as I painted my memories of you on every wall of every floor,

Stopping where you are, *au cinquième étage*, to blind myself with the brushes' sharp ends, so I may see more clearly, see the tracks on the floor,

The killers beneath the bed, the lush trees of Sherbrooke Street, slowly digesting anthocyanin —

And see as you do, Dad, as He sees the geometrically perfect, tear-damp eye of the sparrow.

PAROLE

> Aphasia consists of a breakdown in the two-way translation process
> that establishes a correspondence between thoughts and language...
> *Aphasia is not a disorder of perception.*
> — M. Marsel Mesulam

Neurologists posit a number of steps between a thought and its expression.
In other words, a thought can really *move*,

Stretch out its hamstrings, run in place then leap, landing beyond the cirrus
cloud, inside the geological survey, its grid colour-coded and intact.

Or, it may behave like a drunken slattern at her toilet, atomizing with Avon
Crystal Aura and drawing on her eyebrows with a burnt match;

I am Gloria Gaynor, the thought — originally an ominous MasterCard bill —
spills out of a low-cut, nylon-trimmed rayon slip.

Mid-trip, the thought may change tack or list with ennui, retreating to its
bachelor pad, a cushy, crenellated line —

This is something I talk about with my dad, more or less.

That is, I talk without talking, as he does when the bombs are poised
to detonate, or the cyanide capsules are breaking open in the chamber.

Meaning, naturally, that he is trapped in a violent ward filled with screams
and heavy doors with recessed numerical code-boxes;

That he is blind, and locked also in the dark that spreads like a stain until
everything has been soiled;

And that his words too are captive, on occasion, when they mutate with
memory, emotion impairing their objectivity, as when someone has died

Long ago but it *feels* new and this is not news, I feel the same.

My sister is visiting my parents.
She tells my father that she saw a groundhog at the bus station this morning.

"Where was he going?" he says, thought and language fusing into a key that lets him out and lets us in, and we laugh, it's that simple.

MY LONELINESS EVOLVES

I lost my oldest friend this weekend, by way of an email she signed, Many thanks.

I missed my father's call, too sad, prowled the street, muttering and sick.

When we spoke later on, a patient was in the room telling a long, sibilant story, ending, And now I have to go get a new ticker!

I tried to make him laugh at the man, but *Poor soul* is all he said.

He wanted to hang up because I am so dismal and I became a total brat, saying, I just want to talk to you, God!

He hung up then had my mother call me back.

Your father is all in tears, she said, and he told me that he loves to talk to me, and that he's sorry.

But it's my fault. His clarity is so fine today, as it sometimes is,

As if the illness is the sea, and the fin we are used to seeing changes as he breaches, filling the room with the wonder of his size and beauty.

From my little boat, I saw him today.

And heard his song that sang me to sleep —

Years ago we all sat on my sofa and talked about our similarities.

How are we alike? I asked my dad, and, grabbing my elbow roughly, he said, You are my soul.

How these words are spelled on the foamy surface of the water, in white seaweed and picked-over bones,

How desperately I gather them as he flexes his great tail and jumps, before falling back below as we shake ourselves, saying, Miracle, miracle.

BABY BOY

Is the name of one of the new villains, a thirty-seven-year-old with damp ringlets and tiny, dimpled hands.

The scars on his head are called Oscar and Lipschitt; the dog in the corner, our new dog, is Muldoon.

The Germans make regular appearances, and then the war ends.

On Armistice Day, he is beaten badly by young men we know, who tie him up and attack him with a red-hot curling iron.

The bad men appear regularly, sandwiching the little victories: a football pool, a huge 6/49 win, a sunny, lucky day at the track.

In January I see my father, who has not been eating: there is metal in the food; there are dumps of salt, poison.

Do you know who I am? I say, infuriating him.

I know you, Lynn. Don't worry about that, he says sharply, and I am mortified.

His eyes blaze, sending exigent signals (from an abandoned diphtheria hospital, an *S* flies across the sea).

Three of the men on the floor have died, including Popeye, one woman, Giselle, a great beauty, who often held my hand and asked me to help her,

I'm just so nervous, she would say, quaking. I miss my husband so much.
I am sad about the deaths. Then worried: what if there *is* something in the food?

In their place, a man who plays with baby dolls behind a metal blockade; a man who sings into, and swallows, the outsole of his shoe.

A woman with immense bruises on her face, looking for "my darling father."

Dad, I thought I would write this book as a corollary to your life; that it would elevate you, and end with your recovery.

It occurred to me, too, that you might die and close the cover with a thunk.

Or that I would end when I had nothing left to say about you: that will never happen.

Now, I want to shut this down, to leave you be.

Leave you in one of the lime-green shirts, buried under your blankets and slowly falling asleep.

Leave the coarse brown drapes open for the light; leave and close the door quietly; watch your eyes snap open, then fall, sadly, shut.

And go back to what is left of my own life.

I will think of you, in fragments prefixed by *Never again*; murder these thoughts immediately.

I will colour in 12:20 and 5:15, when we talk, as OCCUPIED, and forget and remember you more and more, because of the growing drift between us,

Between my father, who is the sun, and my father, one of the sun's frail beams, resting pallidly on a quilted pallet.

I know who you are too, Dad, don't worry about that.

And I know what they have done to you, what we have done: each time you pass your hand over your head and ask, again, where the scars are from

Or why are you there, and why can't you leave.

All of my dreams of rescuing you have died. Never again — I stay up and get up very late.

I speak to no one, and do very little.

Frank's cancer is moving inside him, ravenously: we sleep a lot, I talk to him; I watch his legs churn as he dreams of running fast.

Time is standing still, gathering its breath.

I'll see you soon, in Heaven, you say, sometimes. I am closing my eyes watching you bat planets around in a Beastie Boys T-shirt and long shorts,

As my little dog chases and catches them, and won't let go.

Where have you been? you say, and I walk to you, slowly, because there is time; and because there is time, I want you to talk, and I want to listen.

Tell me everything, I say, and you smile.

AFTERWORD

Many years ago, my mother told me that she once said something critical about my father's father, who was no longer alive.

"He isn't here to defend himself," my father said, which my mother took to heart.

My father is very much here, yet he cannot read these poems, and I extend these words as a prayer and shield:

Dad, I am sorry if anything in here troubles or hurts you.

Thank you for writing this book with me. The best parts are all you, everything is you, taking care of me still.

Photograph: Douglas and Lynn Crosbie, 1963.

ACKNOWLEDGEMENTS

In March 2016, my dog, Francis, developed a malignant tumour in his throat, and he was given three months to live. The tumour disappeared shortly thereafter, with thanks to the Queen of Heaven, and to my adored friend Sarah Faber, who knit him a lucky scarf. He is now sixteen-and-a-half.

He has good days and bad days. Every day is a blessing.

Frankie is my best friend, and I thank him for his tremendous strength and valour, as well as my cat (the orange-toed Blaze Starr) for her own vast powers.

I wish to thank Damian Rogers for choosing this book, and for supporting it: *Merci pour ta comprehension et amitié.*

Thanks to my editor Sara Peters, who is precise and intelligent, and to whom, as in her own work, art is truly meaningful. (*Bang Bang, Shoot Em Down*: our accidental credo.)

I extend gratitude also to the incomparable Sarah MacLachlan at House of Anansi, for her magical kindness and unwavering support — my regent.

To everyone at Anansi; to Janie, Matt, Neil; to Maria, a new friend and indispensable ally; and to my favourite dog-sitters, the brilliant women who make me feel like a damn queen: Laura and Amelia.

To Stuart Ross, whose proofreading was profoundly helpful; to Heather Sangster, an early reader, whose fine eye caught so much.

To the Ontario and Canada Arts Councils, for their gracious assistance and belief.

To my brother and sister, for their devotion to our father.

To the staff at my father's *hébergement*, all of whom are excellent: thank you, most of all, from my far more limited perspective, to Charlie and Sofi, who are, plainly, lovely and caring people.

To Hartley Barber, my father's best friend, for visiting regularly, and never failing to cheer my Dad, who has yet to forget him, such is his constancy.

And David McGimpsey, for always listening: you're the very best, Hoss.

To my revered mother, my sweetest friend and an excellent reader, who continued to encourage me to write the book because "it is important that people know." I thank you for your strength, courage and love, Mom.

Finally, thank you, Dad. "No one has ever written a poem about *me*," you said the other day, when I told you what I was working on — what a terrible shame, if that is so.

Thank you for naming this book, in an offhand remark — you remain so funny and so fast. And for encouraging me in everything I ever did: "Just work hard at what you choose to do" is all you ever asked of me.

I have worked hard, with wretched pain and with sheer gladness, talking to, thinking of and remembering you.

The lion's share of my gratitude is extended to you, my beloved father.

Et credere in miracula: revenite.

Note: Tiny fragments appear here and there, including St. Wikipedia's definitions. Thanks to, roughly in order, John Donne ×2, a Steve Martin "comedy joke," Ted Hughes, Delmore Schwartz, *Rocky Balboa*, Brian Wilson, the Velvet Underground, the Jackson 5, William Shakespeare, Public Image, Anne Sexton, the Byrds, Al Purdy, Ken Kesey, *Blade Runner*, Kurt Cobain, David Bowie, T.S. Eliot, Elizabeth Bishop.

Some of these poems appeared in Molly Peacock's *Best Canadian Poems*, Scott Griffin's/ Damian Rogers' *Poetry in Voice*, *Brick*, *Highway*, *Matrix*, *Numéro Cinq*, and *The Walrus*.

Lynn Crosbie was born in Montreal and is a cultural critic, author, and poet. A Ph.D. in English literature with a background in visual studies, she teaches at the University of Toronto and the Art Gallery of Ontario. Her books (of poetry and prose) include *Queen Rat, Dorothy L'Amour,* and *Liar.* She is also the author of the controversial book *Paul's Case,* and most recently *Life Is About Losing Everything* and the Trillium Book Award–nominated novel *Where Did You Sleep Last Night.* She is a contributing editor at *Fashion* and a National Magazine Award winner who has written about sports, style, art, and music.